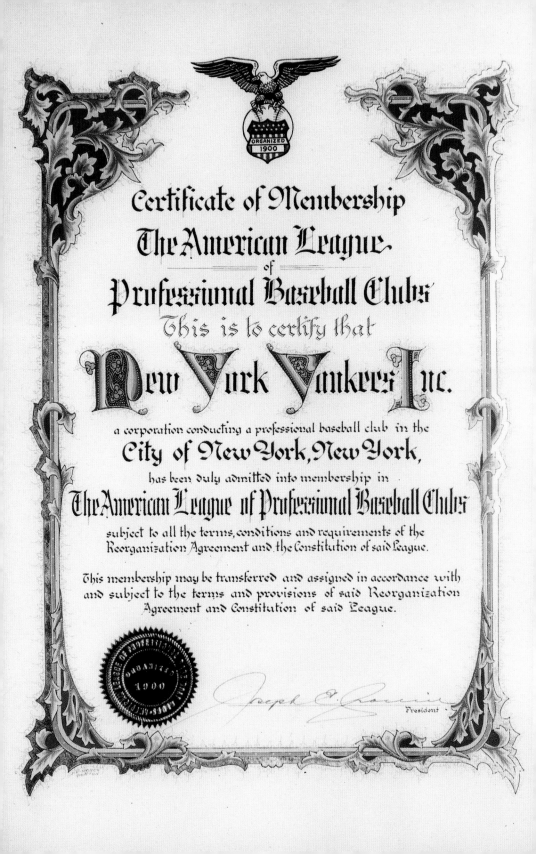

Certificate of Membership

The American League

of

Professional Baseball Clubs

This is to certify that

New York Yankees Inc.

a corporation conducting a professional baseball club in the

City of New York, New York,

has been duly admitted into membership in

The American League of Professional Baseball Clubs

subject to all the terms, conditions and requirements of the
Reorganization Agreement and the Constitution of said League.

This membership may be transferred and assigned in accordance with
and subject to the terms and provisions of said Reorganization
Agreement and Constitution of said League.

President

★★★ THE GREATEST ★★★

# YANKEES TEAMS

★★★ *Featuring* ★★★

## TOP 25 MOMENTS, MARKS AND EVENTS

Selected by the New York–New Jersey Chapter of the Baseball Writers Association of America

Edited by Mark Vancil and Mark Mandrake

RARE AIR BOOKS

Created and Produced by Rare Air Books
A division of Rare Air Media
www.rareairmedia.com

A Ballantine Book
Published by Random House Publishing Group

The Library of Congress Cataloging in Publication Data
is available upon request.

ISBN 0-345-48105-4

Manufactured in the United Kingdom

First Edition: November 2004

9 8 7 6 5 4 3 2 1

# ACKNOWLEDGMENTS

At a moment's notice came an immediate response. What more could be asked of partners, particularly those with multiple responsibilities and limited time? Nothing actually, but that didn't stop anyone connected with this book from lending extra time, insight, talent and kindness to a process already squeezed by narrow schedules and unreasonable demands.

Then again, that's how Major League Baseball's Don Hintze has become the best in his business, and why Mark Mandrake exemplifies the passion and commitment that drives the Yankees. We wouldn't have had a chance without their innate goodness.

At Rare Air Media, Nick DeCarlo never wavered in his pursuit of excellence, even in the hours leading up to his marriage engagement, and Ken Leiker once again answered a call that came at the last minute without a second thought.

And thanks to the professionalism and insight of Anthony Ziccardi, Bill Takes, Jennifer Osborne and Gina Centrello. All publishing experiences should be this fulfilling.

Thanks one and all, including, and not in the least, Laurita, Alexandra, Samantha, Isabella and Jonah. You remain the best of me.

**Mark Vancil – 2004**

To George M. Steinbrenner III, without whom stories of Yankees greatness would be much less great: For a winning tradition the Boss helped restore to sports' most successful team, as well as for the support he has shown me personally and professionally — sincere thanks.

Ever-tolerant Mark Vancil further reinforced his reputation as master juggler and delightful business partner.

Of the Yankee Stadium front office, Al Santasiere, Ken Derry and Glenn Slavin were indispensable on this project. Long nights, early mornings and nonexistent weekends rewarded the continued subjugation of self-interests for this trio. Michael Margolis' editorial alacrity was amazing. Lonn Trost always found a way to squeeze publishing dilemmas into an impossible calendar. Lou Rocco didn't let the photography awards go to his head and grabbed the best shots in the face of adversity.

The interior of this book would have been hollow without cooperation of the ballplayers, managers, and coaches — most particularly Joe Torre, Reggie Jackson, Whitey Ford, Don Mattingly, Goose Gossage, Willie Randolph, Derek Jeter, Paul O'Neill, and Bobby Murcer — whose insights and narrative skills shaped many of these pages. Yogi Berra and Phil Rizzuto lent us not only their collaboration, but that of their grandchildren: Gretchen Berra, Lindsay Berra and Jennifer Rizzuto Congregane.

It's tough to summarize in a few sentences the continued patience shown by my family through the bedlam of recent years. With a Mandrakean (not to mention Yankees-like) flair for high drama, my beautiful daughter Violet Veronica entered the world at the conclusion of the deciding game of the 2003 World Series. Since that day, Violet has proved a blessing to my productivity and the highest inspiration to completing assignments. Heartfelt appreciation also goes to Hanley, Melissa, Janet, and particularly to Jackie — still my wife and my life.

## SPECIAL THANKS

W.C. Burdick, Brad Horn, Jeff Idelson, and Scot Mondore at the National Baseball Hall of Fame and Museum; Heather Benz, Bob Bowman, Patrick Courtney, Paul Cunningham, Mark Feinsand, Phyllis Merhige, Rich Pilling, and Lindsay Reid at Major League Baseball; former and current Yankees staff Kristen Aiken, Doug Behar, Brian Cashman, Joe Flannino, Howard Grosswirth, Jeff Jackson, Jerry Laveroni, Andra McCartney, Arthur Richman, Jayna Rust, Neil Schwartz, Frank Swaine, Michael Tusiani, and Deborah Tymon; other baseball officials Dick Bresciani, Larry Cancro, Barry Gossage, Steve Green, Marty Greenspun, Michael Huang, Marc Levine, Debbie Matson, Kim Ng, Bernadette Repko, and John SooHoo; Dave Kaplan of the Yogi Berra Museum; Larry Burke and Mark Mravic of Sports Illustrated; empirical thanks to Harris Atkins, Eugenie Bisulco, Jeff Botwinick, John Camilleri, Jaime Collins, Larry Desautels, Minna Edelman, Jackie Feinberg, Dr. Charles V. Hamilton, Jamie Herskowitz, Michael Kinstlinger, Marc Miller, Steve Moscov, Bernie Nuñez, Matt Perachi, Michael Shabsels, Patrice St. John, Robert St. John and Alan Ziegler for their support, advice and friendship.

**Mark Mandrake – 2004**

## PHOTOGRAPHY

Photography except as noted below copyright © Corbis Bettman Archives and Mark Mandrake, Lou Rocco, Bernie Nuñez/New York Yankees

| Tomasso DeRosa | 117 | National Baseball Hall of Fame Library, Cooperstown, NY | 106 |
|---|---|---|---|
| Walter Iooss Jr. | 46, 47, 48, 49 90, 121 | | |
| | | Hy Peskin/TimePix | 20 |

# TABLE *of* CONTENTS

# IN SEARCH OF THE

# RING

## A GREAT TEAM REMAKES ITSELF

For the New York Yankees there are only two outcomes: Either they win the

World Series, or they lose the season. Everything else is just historical filler.

In 2003, the Yankees won 101 games during the regular season and nine

more in the postseason — Two wins short of the World Series championship, far

too many when you are the Yankees. In a sport in which every other team starts

the season hoping to reach the World Series, the Yankees arrive for spring

training *expecting* to win the World Series.

Aaron Boone's home run won
the 2003 American League
pennant for the Yankees.

"You win or you lose — that's it," says Yankees shortstop Derek Jeter.

But the Yankees don't lose for long, especially when they lose the way they did in 2003.

The Florida Marlins, budget-conscious upstarts and decided underdogs when the World Series began, shut out the Yankees in Yankee Stadium — the first time since 1981 that the Yankees had lost a postseason series at home. Even more unacceptable for their demanding fans and owner, George Steinbrenner, the Yankees had now gone three years without adding to their trove of 26 World Series titles, after winning four from 1996 to 2000.

Indeed, the Yankees had been fortunate to survive the seven-game American League Championship Series with Boston, prevailing in the bottom of the 11th inning of the final game on Aaron Boone's home run into the Stadium's left-field bleachers.

But at the news conference after the Game 6 loss in the World Series, the first question posed to manager Joe Torre indicated the incredible expectations that accrue of a team with the highest standard for success.

"In your mind, is this the end of an era for the Yankees?"

Not quite.

Less than 72 hours after the Series ended, Steinbrenner assembled the Yankees braintrust in Tampa to assess the roster and map a road to the 2004 postseason. But as the offseason came into focus, the losses didn't stop when the season did. The Yankees needed three starting pitchers, replacements for Andy Pettitte, Roger Clemens and David Wells, who had accounted for 53 wins during the 2003 regular season. The pitching staff was also in dire need of relievers capable of protecting leads until Mariano Rivera could be given the ball. The

Kevin Brown was one of three
starting pitchers who joined the
Yankees in 2004.

everyday lineup needed a middle-of-the-order run-
producer, someone who lived for the accountability
of batting with runners in scoring position.

For most teams, the loss of three-fifths of
their starting pitching staff would be the start of a
rebuilding process. In the Bronx, it's all about
reloading.

When the Yankees failed to trade for Curt
Schilling, one of the game's most dominant starting pitchers, and he landed with the Red Sox
instead, they acquired Javier Vazquez from the
Montreal Expos. Within hours of Pettitte signing
with his hometown Houston Astros, the Yankees
completed a trade with the Los Angeles Dodgers
for Kevin Brown.

The 27-year-old Vazquez was a rising star, and
the 39-year-old Brown was a tough and fearless
competitor. They joined a rotation that included
veteran Mike Mussina, and Jon Lieber, once a sig-

nificant starter who was coming back from a year's
layoff after arm surgery. For the bullpen, the
Yankees added Paul Quantrill and Tom Gordon,
veterans who pitched capably and had the tem-
perament to handle the pressure that comes with
outsized expectation.

Of the two great hitters on the free-agent
market, the Yankees chose to pursue Gary Sheffield
rather than Vladimir Guerrero, partly because of
concern about Guerrero's chronic back pain and
partly because they thought Sheffield could better
handle playing under the glare of New York.
Sheffield committed to the Yankees for three years
and immediately became the team's most danger-
ous right-handed hitter since Dave Winfield.

"No question," Torre said, "that he wants to be
in that batter's box when the game is on the line."

And that was going to be the remake of the
Yankees for 2004, give or take a few peripheral players.

"We have arguably the best
left side of the infield
IN THE HISTORY OF BASEBALL."

— BRIAN CASHMAN,  YANKEES GENERAL MANAGER

The 1931 Yankees hold the modern major league record for most runs scored in a season, 1,067. This chart compares the regulars on that team to the 2004 Yankees regulars. The statistics for the 2004 Yankees are from the 2003 season.

# 1931 YANKEES REGULARS

|     |              | BA   | R   | HR | RBI |
| --- | ------------ | ---- | --- | -- | --- |
| C   | Bill Dickey  | .327 | 65  | 6  | 78  |
| 1B  | Lou Gehrig   | .341 | 163 | 46 | 184 |
| 2B  | Tony Lazzeri | .267 | 67  | 8  | 43  |
| SS  | Lyn Lary     | .280 | 100 | 10 | 107 |
| 3B  | Joe Sewell   | .302 | 102 | 6  | 64  |
| OF  | Babe Ruth    | 373  | 149 | 46 | 163 |
| OF  | Ben Chapman  | .315 | 120 | 17 | 122 |
| OF  | Earle Combs  | .318 | 120 | 5  | 58  |

# 2004 YANKEES REGULARS

|     |                 | BA   | R   | HR | RBI |
| --- | --------------- | ---- | --- | -- | --- |
| C   | Jorge Posada    | .281 | 83  | 30 | 101 |
| 1B  | Jason Giambi    | .250 | 97  | 41 | 107 |
| 2B  | Miguel Cairo    | .295 | 25  | 3  | 23  |
| SS  | Derek Jeter     | .324 | 87  | 10 | 52  |
| 3B  | Alex Rodriguez  | .298 | 124 | 47 | 118 |
| OF  | Gary Sheffield  | .330 | 126 | 39 | 132 |
| OF  | Bernie Williams | .263 | 77  | 15 | 64  |
| OF  | Hideki Matsui   | .287 | 82  | 16 | 106 |
| DH  | Ruben Sierra    | .270 | 33  | 9  | 43  |

But another opportunity developed, and how it played out explains why the Yankees are in the World Series more often than not, and why the Red Sox rarely get there and haven't won it since 1918. Alex Rodriguez, incredibly wealthy but increasingly frustrated in the employ of the last-place Texas Rangers, appeared to be headed for the Red Sox in December, in exchange for Manny Ramirez. That deal fell through when the Players Association objected to a multimillion dollar reduction in A-Rod's contract.

*Gary Sheffield*

Then one day in mid-January, Aaron Boone went up for a rebound in a pickup basketball game, fell awkwardly, and suffered a torn knee ligament — and suddenly the Yankees were without their starting third baseman. Drew Henson, their third baseman of the future, was gone, too, having forfeited the remainder of his contract in order to pursue a career as an NFL quarterback.

One telephone call for a Boone replacement led to another, and when Rodriguez, a Gold Glove shortstop, was asked if he would agree to play third base for the Yankees, the deal was on. The reigning American League Most Valuable Player, and perhaps the best player in baseball, not only wasn't going to Boston, but he was going to the team that the Red Sox owner once had referred to as the "Evil Empire," so despised were the Yankees in New England.

*Alex Rodriguez (left) and Derek Jeter (right)*

With A-Rod and Jeter, "We have arguably the best left side of the infield in the history of baseball," said Yankees general manager Brian Cashman, always the straight man. The addition of A-Rod, who twice had hit more than 50 home runs in a season, afforded the Yankees a lineup that was capable of scoring 1,000 runs in a season. Jeter, the Yankees captain and spiritual leader, took the moves in stride.

"We always make additions, subtractions; we do all kinds of things," he said. "So you wait until spring training to see what team you have. But one thing's always the same: You're sure we're going to have an opportunity to win again. That's just the way things are done around here."

# TEAMS THAT DEFINED THE ERAS
## IN MORE THAN A
# CENTURY *of* EXCELLENCE

### JOE DiMAGGIO'S LASTING PRESENCE
*— Essay by Donald Honig*

### FIVE OUT OF 100

### THE MANAGERS

*Any attempt to select or define the greatest individual team in baseball*

*history must start with the New York Yankees. For most of the 20th Century,*

*the debate rested with the 1927 Yankees of Babe Ruth and Lou Gehrig.*

*More recently the case has been made for Joe DiMaggio's 1939 team.*

*In the opening essay, noted author Donald Honig sets the stage by*

*revisiting DiMaggio and a legend that has never gone out of style.*

*We look at five Yankees teams and make a case for each,*

*including Mickey Mantle's in 1961, Reggie Jackson's in 1978,*

*and the 1998 team of Derek Jeter and Bernie Williams.*

AL
MOST VALUABLE PLAYER
1939 1941
1947
AL
RBI LEADER
1938
1939 AL
BATTING CHAMPION
1941 1918
1939
CONSECUTIVE
GAMES WITH A HIT
**56**
1940
1937 1937
1948
AL
HOME RUN CHAMPION
1940
1937 1941
AL
RUNS SCORED LEADER
TOTAL BASES LEADER
AL

*Yankee Clipper*

# JOE DiMAGGIO'S
## LASTING PRESENCE

### *Essay by Donald Honig*

In March 1998, *Time* magazine observed the 75th anniversary of its founding. To mark the occasion, Time, Inc., arranged a dinner and invited some 1,200 of the world's most notable personalities. The guests, many of whom had graced the cover of *Time*, included the most renowned names from the spheres of arts and letters, politics, medicine, science, athletics and entertainment. No less a venue than Radio City Music Hall was procured to accommodate the gathering.

The guest list included then-President Clinton, Henry Kissinger, Mikhail Gorbachev, Muhammad Ali, Bill Gates, Sophia Loren, Tom Cruise, Steven Spielberg, Walter Cronkite, an array of Nobel Prize winners and just about anyone else whose achievement had illuminated some corner of the globe. Never before had such an assemblage of glamour, glitter, and accomplishment been gathered under one roof. Toasts were made as luminary upon luminary of the earthly firmament rose to honor one another.

It fell on actor Kevin Costner to toast a man who had done little of note for nearly half a century, yet Costner had no trouble hitting the mark with his introduction:

"Men like Joe DiMaggio," Costner said, "are not just of their own time. They are men for the ages. And as the century comes to a close, and debates heat about who is the man or woman of the century, I know the list will be impressive. But it will not be complete unless Joe DiMaggio's name is on it. So I'd like you to raise a glass to Joe DiMaggio, for showing us the way."

And more than a thousand of the world's elite rose to their feet and accorded an 83-year-old, long-retired baseball player the evening's "longest and most thunderous ovation," newspapers reported the following day. It is doubtful that, except for his 56-game hitting streak in 1941, many of the august crowd at Radio City Music Hall could have recited the statistics that had brought the frail, silver-haired old slugger to eminence in the first place. Not his .381 batting title in 1939 (unmatched by any right-handed hitter since); not his 167 RBI in 1937; not his .325 lifetime batting average; not his astonishingly meager 13 strikeouts in 1941 (about one for every 42 at-bats). The truth was that the man, the persona, had long-since transcended his celebrated statistics and grown into the perfect fit for the nation's image of a hero.

In reference to that remarkable paucity of strikeouts, Yankees pitcher Vic Raschi once made a statement that unwittingly served as a metaphor for DiMaggio himself. "For a power hitter," Raschi said, "Joe had an incredible eye. He had an uncanny talent for making contact."

In DiMaggio's case the "uncanny talent" for making contact extended far beyond the pitched ball, beyond the observable exploits, beyond the playing days. It went on and on, in the public mind forever undiminished and untarnished. In the retired baseball player, the national imagination sensed something that it wanted, perhaps felt it needed, and elevated him to a plateau where the ovations would always be the "longest and most thunderous."

The irony lies in the fact that the man who was able to make "contact" with and evoke such adulation among legions of admirers for decade after decade had a remote, undemonstrative personality. His seedbed was baseball, of course, the national game. But there are few truly legendary baseball figures, and diamond heroics alone will not insure a place in the country's mythology.

Among baseball's enduring legends, personalities vary. There is no prototype. The grandest of all

is Babe Ruth, the man DiMaggio came to replace in the skies over Yankee Stadium. Ruth was a noisy extrovert, crude and lovable. He has been described as "Moby Dick in a goldfish bowl." He roared through life with the orgiastic appetites of a Roman emperor. There was no mystery to Ruth. Set him to music and he was "The 1812 Overture."

No less loved and idolized, Ruth's successor and he could not have been more unalike. DiMaggio was different from all other diamond legends. Ty Cobb was a taut wire of snarls and ferocity. Honus Wagner was modest and folksy. Walter Johnson was the humble epitome of American virtues. Dizzy Dean was cornball witty and boastful. With all his mighty power, Lou Gehrig lacked electricity — he was immediately overshadowed in 1936 by the rookie DiMaggio — and gained legendary status through tragedy. Willie Mays was a bubbly personality who seemed to embody the game's spirit of eternal youth. The near-flawless hitter Ted Williams was known during his career for his explosive temper. Mickey Mantle was a Hercules of baseball talent.

All of them part of our folklore, yet the essential renown of each was gained solely through their baseball careers. It was DiMaggio who took his fame further, without noise, wit, theatrics, or discernible "personality." DiMaggio alone seemed to fit an ideal and have a status conferred upon him. He came as close to royalty as a democratic nation allows.

How did he do this? "He did it by doing nothing," sportswriter Red Smith said. "By that I mean nothing except be Joe DiMaggio. He simply perpetuated that plain fact. I'm afraid you have to resort to hyperbole to describe the impact he had on people." Smith recalled a walk he took with DiMaggio from a New York nightclub to a hotel where yet another testimonial dinner awaited. "The gawking and the gasping he evoked in a cynical, seen-it-all city had to be experienced to be believed," Smith said. "Cab drivers yelled to him and almost drove into the plateglass windows because they couldn't take their eyes off him. People just stopped dead in their tracks and stared at him. It was a modest whiff of what the Second Coming might be like. I never felt more invisible than when I was in Joe's company."

On the field, DiMaggio was as zealously competitive as Cobb was at his most ferocious self. But the man who came to stylize baseball, as it had never been before, did it with a quiet intensity that kept all eyes riveted on him. What inner demons possessed him were not for public display, to the extent that his lone display of emotion on a baseball field was considered notable and is often replayed on highlight reels.

The display occurred at Yankee Stadium in the sixth game of the 1947 World Series, Yankees

DiMaggio's reticence impressed itself upon his teammates more than any exclamatory outbursts would have.

"Joe was a good teammate," said pitcher Spud Chandler. "He was quiet but not silent, if you know what I mean. You knew when he was around. I always said I could have walked into the Yankees clubhouse blindfolded and told you whether Joe was there or not. That's what he did: create an atmosphere. The mood was different, the talk was different. We were in awe of him, but he never put himself up on a pedestal. He was always approachable. If you needed a favor, like tickets for a hit Broadway show, he'd get them for you. Joe

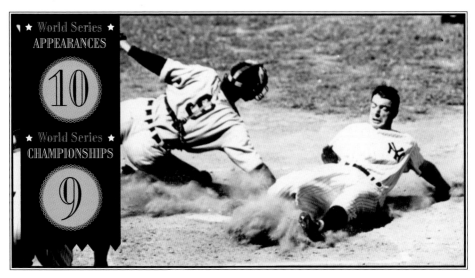

versus Dodgers. DiMaggio tore into a pitch and sent a throbbing drive to deep left field that looked for sure to be a game-tying, three-run home run. He certainly believed the ball had sufficient carry. But Dodgers left fielder Al Gionfriddo, in the breathless words of announcer Red Barber, went "back, back, back, back, back" and made a spectacular grab at the wall. DiMaggio was approaching second base when he saw the catch being made. It was then that he allowed his memorable, uncharacteristic display of emotion: a brief, frustrated kick at the ground. For many people this slight fissure in an otherwise wall of stoic resolve remains as graphic as Gionfriddo's catch.

knew all the big shots in town."

They all said he was the perfect teammate, one who never considered himself different from anyone else. He asked only one thing of his fellow Yankees: professionalism. For DiMaggio that meant playing to win, all the time.

"If he didn't think you were bearing down on the field," Chandler said, "God help you."

DiMaggio's rancor was in character. "He wouldn't say anything," Chandler said. "But you'd get into the dugout and find him frowning at you. Believe me, it made you shrivel."

"He played with a streak of fire in him," Vic Raschi said. "It was pride. I think he took more pride in his game than any player I ever saw."

When asked why he played with such unremitting fervor, even at times when the score did not demand it, DiMaggio's oft-quoted answer was: "There is always some kid who may be seeing me for the first or last time, I owe him my best."

The answer is an insight into the man: The impression he left on the mind of every nameless stranger who was watching him was important. The leader's responsibility was unceasing. He remained faithful to this creed for all his days.

DiMaggio brought his star qualities to New York in 1936. The most acclaimed player in the minor leagues, he had excelled with his hometown San Francisco Seals, for whom he achieved a harbinger streak of hitting safely in 61 consecutive games

DiMaggio had attained iconic status. The shy, at times almost wary son of an immigrant Sicilian fisherman came to feel at home in the most dynamic and sophisticated city in America. From the time he arrived in New York, when baseball was still almost exclusively a daylight game, the new man chose to spend his evenings in places like Toots Shor's restaurant or the high-profile Stork Club, in the company of the city's most popular, colorful, and powerful politicians, entertainers, journalists, columnists (most especially the influential Walter Winchell), Broadway characters, and an amorphous species known in those days as "sportsmen."

The apotheosis of Joe DiMaggio began on those long, smoky nights, far from the San

### 1936 SAN FRANCISCO SEALS

#### ⚜ MOST VALUABLE PLAYER SEASON TOTALS ⚜

| Games | At Bats | Hits | Runs | RBI | Average |
|-------|---------|------|------|-----|---------|
| 172 | 679 | 270 | 173 | 154 | .398* |

| Doubles | Triples | Home Runs | ■ Led league |
|---------|---------|-----------|--------------|
| 48 | 18 | 34 | *Lost batting title by a point to Oscar Eckhardt |

in 1933. A knee injury in 1934 made him suspect, and major league teams backed away from the heavy price tag Seals ownership had placed on him. The Yankees, however, took a gamble and obtained DiMaggio's contract in exchange for $25,000 — no small sum in those Depression years — and five players. A proviso in the deal was that the 20-year-old center fielder remain with the Seals for the 1935 season. Playing in the elongated Pacific Coast League season — Joe appeared in 172 games — he collected 270 hits and batted .398. On that wave he rode into New York, proclaimed by an anticipatory New York press as the heir to Ruth, who had left the Yankees two years earlier.

No rookie had ever entered the major leagues faced with such expectations, and no rookie had so instantly and lavishly fulfilled them. By 1939,

Francisco wharves of his childhood, far from the Sicilian culture brought across the Atlantic and then transcontinentally by his fisherman father, who by some genetic quirk raised a trio of baseball players from among his nine children (Joe's brothers Dominic and Vince would follow him to the major leagues). Ironically, the man born to become the sleekest ship of state ever to make passage across the green grass of America's outfields was subject to bouts of sea sickness when working aboard his father's boat, an early, telltale sign of where the young man's destiny lay.

DiMaggio's range of associations grew exponentially. He was a brilliant young star who possessed a special magic on the field and off, and the famous, always drawn to their kind, vied to sit in his reflected glory. Sportswriters sensed something unique had entered the tent and found in the reserved young ballplayer a fascinating subject, one whose self-protective screen made him even more intriguing.

"He was quiet, almost inarticulate in those years," Red Smith said. "He sat among a lot of the lions of the day, but looking back I don't think Joe was ever awed by anybody. That shoe was on the other foot. Joe created his own magnetic field right from the beginning. He saw how people reacted to him and he just built his own sense of who he was, and that it was more than just being a ballplayer. With some kids — and that's what he was then, remember — this sort of fawning and outright sycophancy increases the head size by quantum leaps. But with Joe you got the feeling he was absorbing it very carefully. Outside of what he did when he had spikes on his feet you couldn't really define him. Successful young men tend to transparency, but not this one.

*Lou Gehrig and Joe DiMaggio.*

"Joe had what you might describe as a 'shrewd silence.' I wouldn't call him a student of human nature. Something else perhaps. A student of fame and the famous. I think he knew he was in it for the long haul and was learning how to conduct himself."

This makes the young DiMaggio sound somewhat calculating, but more likely he was following natural instincts, focusing on self-involvement with the same diligence that he focused on the ballfield. Yankees pitcher Eddie Lopat recalled being the beneficiary of DiMaggio's brand of concentration.

"What made me realize just how great DiMaggio was," Lopat said, "was something that happened during a game I was pitching in New York against Cleveland in 1948, my first year with the Yankees. We were winning by either 2-1 or 3-2. I had two men on and two out and Lou Boudreau was up. In spots like that I would sometimes turn my back on the hitter and do a little thinking about how to start him off. I noticed Joe out there, playing straightaway in center. Then I turned around, got my sign, and threw the first pitch. It was a ball. When I got the ball back I turned around again, mumbling to myself, and there's Joe out in dead center. The next pitch was ball two. Now I was really upset with myself and didn't turn around.

"I threw the next pitch and Boudreau stepped in and creamed it. He sent a line drive over Rizzuto's head. One of those vicious long line drives. The moment that ball left the bat I knew it was ticketed. Right into the left-center slot. A sure triple and two runs. When I turned around Joe was standing there, catching the ball without ever having moved. I was shocked, frankly.

"When we got into the dugout after the inning I sat down next to him. 'Joe,' I said, 'I noticed you were in dead center on the first couple of pitches. But then he hits the ball flush into the gap and you're standing right there.'

" 'Well,' he said, 'I've seen you pitch enough times now to know how you work. I knew that as long as you stayed ahead of him or were even you wouldn't let him pull the ball. But when you went

# 56-GAME DAY-BY-DAY

| DATE | HITS | TEAM | DATE | HITS | TEAM |
|------|------|------|------|------|------|
| May 15 | 1-for-4 | Chicago | June 16 | 1-for-5 | Cleveland |
| May 16 | 2-for-4 | Chicago | June 17 | 1-for-4 | Chicago |
| May 17 | 1-for-3 | Chicago | June 18 | 1-for-3 | Chicago |
| May 18 | 3-for-3 | St. Louis | June 19 | 3-for-3 | Chicago |
| May 19 | 1-for-3 | St. Louis | June 20 | 4-for-5 | Detroit |
| May 20 | 1-for-5 | St. Louis | June 21 | 1-for-4 | Detroit |
| May 21 | 2-for-5 | Detroit | June 22 | 2-for-5 | Detroit |
| May 22 | 1-for-4 | Detroit | June 24 | 1-for-4 | St. Louis |
| May 23 | 1-for-5 | Boston | June 25 | 1-for-4 | St. Louis |
| May 24 | 1-for-4 | Boston | June 26 | 1-for-4 | St. Louis |
| May 25 | 1-for-4 | Boston | June 27 | 2-for-3 | Philadelphia |
| May 27 | 4-for-5 | Washington | June 28 | 2-for-5 | Philadelphia |
| May 28 | 1-for-4 | Washington | June 29 | 1-for-4 | Washington |
| May 29 | 1-for-3 | Washington | June 29 | 1-for-5 | Washington |
| May 30 | 1-for-3 | Boston | July 1 | 2-for-4 | Boston |
| May 30 | 1-for-4 | Boston | July 1 | 1-for-3 | Boston |
| June 1 | 1-for-4 | Cleveland | July 2 | 1-for-5 | Boston |
| June 1 | 1-for-4 | Cleveland | July 5 | 1-for-4 | Philadelphia |
| June 2 | 2-for-4 | Cleveland | July 6 | 4-for-5 | Philadelphia |
| June 3 | 1-for-4 | Detroit | July 6 | 2-for-4 | Philadelphia |
| June 5 | 1-for-5 | Detroit | July 10 | 1-for-2 | St. Louis |
| June 7 | 3-for-5 | St. Louis | July 11 | 4-for-5 | St. Louis |
| June 8 | 2-for-4 | St. Louis | July 12 | 2-for-5 | St. Louis |
| June 8 | 2-for-4 | St. Louis | July 13 | 3-for-4 | Chicago |
| June 10 | 1-for-5 | Chicago | July 13 | 1-for-4 | Chicago |
| June 12 | 2-for-4 | Chicago | July 14 | 1-for-3 | Chicago |
| June 14 | 1-for-2 | Cleveland | July 15 | 2-for-4 | Chicago |
| June 15 | 1-for-3 | Cleveland | July 16 | 3-for-4 | Cleveland |

**TOTALS**

| AVG | AB | R | H | 2B | 3B | HR | RBI |
|-----|-----|-----|-----|-----|-----|-----|-----|
| .408 | 223 | 56 | 91 | 16 | 4 | 15 | 55 |

behind two balls and no strikes, I knew you had to get the next one over and that he knew it too and would probably pull it.'

"Do you know how far over he moved before I threw that pitch? About 80 feet.

"So I said to him, 'That was great thinking, Joe.' And do you know what? He just turned away from me with kind of a scowl. He didn't want to be complimented. I guess he just thought it was his job to do the right thing, that that was what was expected of him."

The specialness that was DiMaggio was immediately apparent to his Yankees teammates. Although he was often open and congenial with them, he also could be aloof and private, sitting alone in an enigmatic silence. The latter moods disturbed no one.

*DiMaggio managed a weary smile and made zeros with his fingers and thumbs after his 56-game hitting streak came to an end on July 16, 1941.*

"He was revered in that clubhouse," Spud Chandler said. "He was so dedicated and splendid a player that we all recognized the fact that he was different, and it got to the point where we wanted him to be different. So if he was moody now and then and didn't always hang around with the boys, that was all right. We expected it. He was different, you see."

As .406 is to the legend of Ted Williams, so the 56-game hitting streak is to DiMaggio. The streak is the perfect metaphor for the man: a pressure-ridden run of high-caliber consistency. It is DiMaggio's career vibrantly encapsulated. As the streak gradually extended into headline-making proportions, the daily pressure must have been excruciating.

"You'd watch him before one of those games and you couldn't help wondering what he was thinking," said catcher Bill Dickey. "Of course there wasn't much talk about it in the clubhouse. You just didn't want to mention it, like with a pitcher who has a late-inning no-hitter going. Naturally the streak was on Joe's mind. But it never showed."

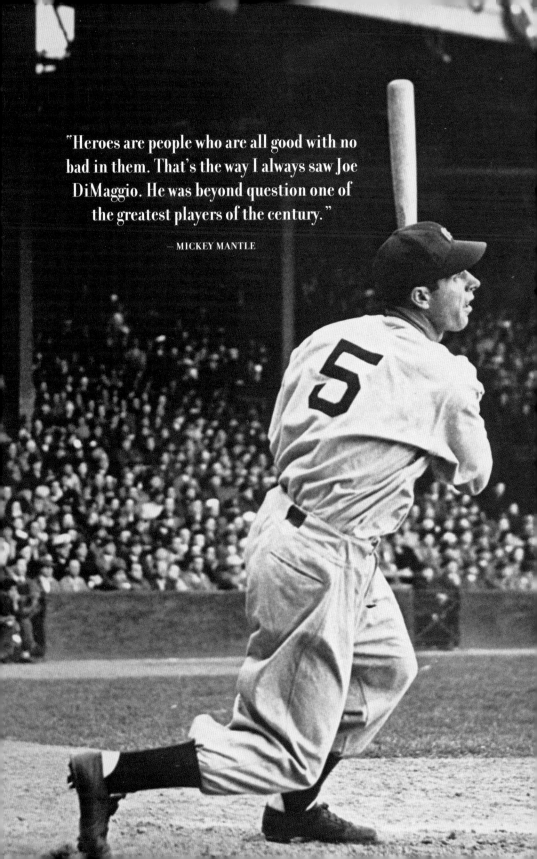

"Heroes are people who are all good with no bad in them. That's the way I always saw Joe DiMaggio. He was beyond question one of the greatest players of the century."

— MICKEY MANTLE

It never showed. Always the guarded demeanor. As the hitting streak grew to epic proportions, DiMaggio knew what everyone in the ballpark was thinking about and waiting to see. It was hard enough in normal circumstances to go out there knowing he was expected to be the star performer; but when he knew that everything was focused on each swing of his bat, the pressure must have gone to extremes. Fulfilling those daily expectations was as great a demand as any athlete has ever faced. And DiMaggio went on, shattering old records and setting new ones as he sculpted what is the most extended, thrillingly heroic one-man feat in all sports.

"A long hitting streak is sustained by control," said Joe McCarthy, the Yankees manager in the DiMaggio era. "And Joe had that. He had to have it. You can't go up to the plate in those situations being overanxious. You go up there knowing what you have to do, then wait patiently to do it. Even if it's late in the game and you don't have your hit yet. That was Joe. That's what made him the perfect player. Joe was the perfect player."

That self-control was to help make him the perfect hero. From the field he carried it with him everywhere. Perhaps the most remarkable thing about DiMaggio was the unfaltering longevity of his celebrity. The ovation at the *Time* dinner near the end of his life tells us that it never diminished; in an era of perishable fame, DiMaggio's legacy would forever endure.

He had long since attained mythic proportions and had to do nothing to extol himself. He had merely to maintain the impeccability of being Joe DiMaggio; the rest was conferred. His mere appearance was his coin and he was conscious of it, always outfitted in custom-made suits and overcoats. If the public had an image of him, he made sure not to blur it. He remained the embodiment of old glories tailored in grace, style, dignity — the flesh and blood representation of the American hero.

The genuine and unending esteem of millions, for decades, is a recipe for swollen ego. If DiMaggio fell victim to this human failing it was never apparent to those who came to fete him. He seemed to have effortlessly adapted himself to cheers, applause, beaming faces, to have absorbed it all rather than allow it to resonate within him. His responses were studies in long-honed instinct. There was no excess of humility, just the magic name, the familiar trimly tailored figure, raising his hand and sending out a greeting with a slight twirl of his fingers. (Whether Joe knew it or not, the gesture was similar to that offered crowds from the balcony of Buckingham Palace by Great Britain's wartime King George VI.)

But there was another DiMaggio, one all too sensitive to his man-on-a-pedestal stature, a condition that now and then could nag at him. On one occasion he had accepted an invitation to attend a testimonial dinner on the West Coast. Delegated to meet him at the airport and shepherd him to his accommodations was Bobby Bragan, former major league player and future major league manager, then managing the Hollywood Stars of the Pacific Coast League.

"Somebody else had booked the motel," Bragan said, "and had screwed up royally. When we got there I was appalled. It was a third-rate place off the highway. You know, one of those places with a blinking neon sign with one of the letters crashed out. I was embarrassed, and I apologized to Joe and offered to take him to a more upscale place. But he said, 'For Christ's sake, Bobby, all I want is a bed to sleep in. What the hell's the difference?' When we walked in to register, the clerk almost fell over. Joe gave him an autograph and went to sleep. That's the Joe I knew."

On another occasion — this was in the 1970s — DiMaggio was one of the celebrities at a Jimmy Fund golf tournament at a course outside Hartford. To help publicize the event, he agreed to an interview with Arnold Dean, the area's widely admired sports talk show host. Dean was broadcasting from a makeshift studio set up in the upstairs of a small building at the edge of the course.

"Joe showed up just before the top of the hour," Dean said, "which meant we had about a

10-minute wait until the news had been read. He said that was fine with him and he took a seat. The next thing I knew some people were calling his name and making a fuss outside. There was a sliding door that opened onto a portico and I went out to have a look. About 15 or 20 people had gathered below and were calling for him.

"I knew Joe was very shy, especially when it came to the unexpected. When I came back in and told him what was going on down there, he got up and went outside and waved to the people and posed for pictures, all very good-naturedly.

"I guess word had got around that Joe DiMaggio was there and was posing for pictures, because when we finally finished the interview there was quite a hubbub outside. When I looked out again I was taken aback — there must have been well over 100 people gathered, all shouting for Joe. I guess I was kind of embarrassed; I'd gotten the poor guy into more than he'd bargained for. He asked me how many people were down there, and I gave him my estimate.

" 'Look,' he said, 'I'm not going to go out there again. It makes me very uncomfortable to be standing somewhere looking down at people. Hell, I'm not the Pope.'

"What he did," Dean said, "was go downstairs and plunge right into that crowd, shaking hands, signing autographs, posing for pictures. I don't know if he enjoyed it or not. I doubt it. But he did it, and graciously. Because he felt uncomfortable looking down at them."

This was the same man who as a ballplayer would sometimes sit for hours in the Yankees clubhouse after a game until he knew the crowds waiting outside for him had broken up and gone away, the same man who could freeze intrusive strangers with a glare and who had a natural predisposition for privacy.

Contradictory? Perhaps, but understandably, for throughout his long years of fame the man faced many varied, and sometimes whimsically unexpected, things.

DiMaggio would now and then attend the annual induction ceremonies at the Baseball Hall of Fame in Cooperstown, N.Y. On one

"There is always some kid who may be seeing me for the first or last time. I owe him my best."

— JOE DiMAGGIO

of those occasions, seeking a few hours' respite, he and a companion went for a drive through the countryside. The two men soon found themselves lost on a remote country road. Seeing a farmer riding his tractor in a nearby field, they stopped and signaled the man over to ask for directions.

"The guy was very obliging," the companion said. "He climbed down from the tractor and came over to the car and leaned his elbow on the window and found himself face to face with Joe DiMaggio. I asked him for directions and he gave them, never taking his eyes off Joe the whole time. I thanked him, but he wasn't finished. He had a favor to ask: Would Joe mind stepping out and autographing his tractor? Joe looked at me with that poker face of his, then got out and followed the guy across the field. I'll never forget the sight of Joe, in his beautifully tailored suit, following that guy in overalls and floppy hat across the field, where he autographed the tractor. They shook hands and Joe came back to the car. When he had settled himself in, he said, 'I've autographed pictures, bats, balls, gloves, menus,

you name it … 'He didn't have to finish the sentence. But somewhere in upstate New York there's a guy driving around on a tractor autographed by Joe DiMaggio."

When Ted Williams, DiMaggio's lone contemporary rival for diamond supremacy, died in July 2002, the admiring tributes mentioned Williams having missed nearly five prime seasons to military service, with dreamy speculation about what his record might have looked like had he played in those years. DiMaggio likewise lost prime years — from 1943 through 1945 — to military service, but baseball fantasists seldom try to fill them in. DiMaggio, it seems, always has been seen as complete, in need of no enhancements, no what-ifs, because his record needs no embellishment.

The man to whom DiMaggio's Yankees torch was passed also possessed extraordinary post-career charisma. Within the hierarchy of retired athletes, Mickey Mantle was indeed a close rival of DiMaggio's in popularity. Some fans, in fact, saw Mantle as the superior player, citing his greater power (from both sides of the

"Joe was the loneliest man I ever knew.
He couldn't even eat a meal in a hotel restaurant, the fans just
wouldn't let him. He led the league in room service."

— EDDIE LOPAT, DiMaggio's teammate, 1948–1951

plate) and blinding foot speed. The debates could be fervent, but as far as the long-term public consciousness was concerned, they were irrelevant, because immense though Mantle's accomplishments had been, they had been built upon perishables: power and speed. They left behind awe and magical memories, but what Mantle always evoked was baseball — baseball of Ruthian might, yes, but only baseball — whereas DiMaggio had excelled at championship baseball and then carried on through decades of tumultuous social change like a talisman of the old and the good. The eminent Yankee had been anointed as the connection between past and present, the repository of standards and ideals whose decline many felt had a negative effect on the national health.

What flaws and shortcomings DiMaggio might have had did not matter; they were mere scratches on a sculpture, from a distance invisible. He could be brusque, aloof, demanding — the perfect hero could be at times all too human. That he

also could be generous, loyal, and giving were likewise of no relevance, for these too were human qualities and of little interest to an adoring public. An idealization had occurred, and that was that.

DiMaggio was to be raised even higher in the public imagination by his second marriage, to Marilyn Monroe, who was to undergo her own apotheosis. The short-lived marriage — it lasted about a year — was to be woven forever into the tapestry of the DiMaggio mystique. It was more a collision of headlines than a marriage, a hard bumping of two distinct and ultimately incompatible legends. Two antithetical personalities: she insecure and flashy, he a study in self-control. Whatever the initial expectations they brought to the union, whatever love, affection, and need, it was doomed. She could not change; he would not.

He accepted her untimely death with a soundless mourning that ceased only with the moment of his own passing. Never did the inner man come more to the surface than with Marilyn's death. Her name was not to be mentioned in his presence, except by himself, and then only to intimate friends.

"He would occasionally mention her," one of those friends said. "It was usually in bitter, resentful terms about those whom he felt had betrayed and exploited her, like the Kennedys or Sinatra. Those conversations were always one-sided; you knew enough not to ask questions. He just had to let it out now and then."

When the editor-in-chief of a large New York publishing house met DiMaggio on a social occasion and offered him "a blank check" for his autobiography, DiMaggio, knowing what revelations such a book must include, declined.

"He was polite," the editor said, "but in a way that told me it would be futile to pursue it."

Asked if he was disappointed, the editor indicated his own fascination with the DiMaggio image. "I was disappointed that he said no," the editor said, "but I think I might have been more disappointed had he said yes."

That DiMaggio was willing to forgo seven-figure publishing deals if accepting them meant he had to drop the veils of his privacy and that of his fabled ex-wife is an insight into the man and the code he lived by. In an age of lurid and shameless tell-all, his was the rare principled silence.

His fame had reached an apogee and there it remained, never to decline. At Old-Timers games all introductions ended with "The Man They Saved for Last," when his appearance and the roaring ovation it evoked seemed to place an official stamp on the event. He was named "The Greatest Living Player," but even that impressive accolade defined him only partially. Years ago, Yankees pitcher and close DiMaggio friend Lefty Gomez whimsically described his teammate as "mysterious." And mysterious DiMaggio remained, and that the mystery was never solved did not seem to matter.

Presidents fawned over him. He attended the big prizefights with Ernest Hemingway (who had referred to "the great DiMaggio" in his novella *The*

*Old Man and the Sea*). Henry Kissinger couldn't believe that one day "I would be friends with DiMaggio."

Why DiMaggio, and not Mays or Williams, players of equal stature? Maybe because DiMaggio was "mysterious." To the public eye he had begun that way and had never changed. Trying to put him in larger context, one writer wrote that DiMaggio had become "a symbol to hang on to and cherish, a man from the old, strong, flawless America when Franklin Roosevelt was president and Joe Louis was heavyweight champion and Clark Gable was the king of Hollywood and Ernest Hemingway was shooting lions in Africa."

How would DiMaggio be seen if he were playing today, subjected to a more prying, less deferential media? One has to wonder at his reaction to ceaseless barrages of microphones, tape recorders, camcorders, pointed questions by insistent writers. It is unlikely that this guarded man would have been any different. He would be cooperative to a point, and beyond that the media would have to adapt, accepting his supreme talents as the ultimate point of contact.

Among today's often excessively exuberant, high-fiving heroes, DiMaggio would appear, as he always did, unique. And perhaps his would be the style, the uncompromising professionalism, that young players would seek to emulate, that the man who had set not only records but standards years ago would have done so today.

As time went on and DiMaggio aged, the feeling that we weren't going to see his kind again become more pervasive. The accolades grew more heartfelt, the applause more fervent, as though we were seeing off the man and what he represented. DiMaggio was going to take it all with him, as well he might, for there was no one to replace him.

Yankees pitcher Spud Chandler once recalled, "Just before the first pitch of every game I would turn around and look out to center field. I liked the feeling of seeing him out there. You don't know what a good feeling that was."

# 1927

In October 1927, longtime Brooklyn Dodgers manager Wilbert Robinson expressed the opinion that the 1927 Yankees were the greatest baseball team of all time. Hearing this, longtime New York Giants manager John McGraw yelped and jumped about three feet into the air.

A little background: Robinson and McGraw were teammates on the Baltimore Orioles in the 1890s and best of friends for years after that. McGraw became manager of the Giants in 1902. When Robinson in 1914 was hired to manage the Dodgers, the two men began to quarrel and feud.

By 1927, McGraw had spent 10 years trying to convince baseball writers that the 1894 Baltimore Orioles were the greatest baseball team ever put together. When Robinson expressed the opinion that the 1927 Yankees were the greatest team ever, perhaps he truly believed it, or perhaps it was an attempt to undermine McGraw's campaign for the 1894 Orioles. Sportswriters dwelled on the topic for a month or so, and after that, the idea that the 1927 Yankees were the greatest team ever was well established in the public's mind. The Yankees went 110-44, winning the pennant by 19 games and won the World Series in 4 games.

But were they really the best ever? One method of considering this issue is to break the large, general question into smaller, more specific questions that might be more conducive to objective study.

**1) Has there ever been a team, aside from the 1927 Yankees, that has had two stars of the magnitude of Babe Ruth and Lou Gehrig, both with big seasons?**

Yes. In the 19th Century there were several teams that had two pitchers who would win about 35 games each and play the outfield when they weren't pitching. The

## 1927 ROSTER

### THE REGULARS

| | | G | R | H | HR | RBI | BA | OBP |
|---|---|---|---|---|---|---|---|---|
| C | Pat Collins | 92 | 38 | 69 | 7 | 36 | .275 | .407 |
| 1B | Lou Gehrig | 155 | 149 | 218 | 47 | 175 | .373 | .474 |
| 2B | Tony Lazzeri | 153 | 92 | 176 | 18 | 102 | .309 | .383 |
| 3B | Joe Dugan | 112 | 44 | 104 | 2 | 43 | .269 | .321 |
| SS | Mark Koenig | 123 | 99 | 150 | 3 | 62 | .285 | .320 |
| OF | Earle Combs | 152 | 137 | 231 | 6 | 64 | .356 | .414 |
| OF | Babe Ruth | 151 | 158 | 192 | 60 | 164 | .356 | .486 |
| OF | Bob Meusel | 135 | 75 | 174 | 8 | 103 | .337 | .393 |
| Team | | 155 | 975 | 1,644 | 158 | 908 | .307 | .381 |
| AL rank | | | 1 | 1 | 1 | 1 | 1 | 1 |

### THE ROTATION

| | G | ERA | W | L | SV | IP | SO |
|---|---|---|---|---|---|---|---|
| Waite Hoyt | 36 | 2.63 | 22 | 7 | 1 | 256 | 86 |
| Herb Pennock | 34 | 3.00 | 19 | 8 | 2 | 210 | 51 |
| Urban Shocker | 31 | 2.84 | 18 | 6 | 0 | 200 | 35 |
| Dutch Ruether | 27 | 3.38 | 13 | 6 | 0 | 184 | 45 |
| George Pipgras | 29 | 4.11 | 10 | 3 | 0 | 166 | 81 |

### THE TOP RELIEVERS

| | G | ERA | W | L | SV | IP | SO |
|---|---|---|---|---|---|---|---|
| Wilcy Moore | 50 | 2.28 | 19 | 7 | 13 | 213 | 75 |
| Bob Shawkey | 19 | 2.89 | 2 | 3 | 4 | 44 | 23 |
| Team | 155 | 3.20 | 110 | 44 | 20 | 1,389 | 431 |
| AL rank | | | 1 | 1 | 3 | 2 | 3 |

1886 St. Louis Browns had Bob Caruthers, who went 30-14 as a pitcher and played the outfield the rest of the time and batted .334. His teammate Dave Foutz went 41-16 as a pitcher and also played the outfield and batted .280. Caruthers and Foutz had more impact on the league than Ruth and Gehrig did because the game was very different in their era.

Since 1900, one team has had two players have bigger seasons than Ruth and Gehrig did in 1927. The 1912 Boston Red Sox got a 34-5 record and 1.91 ERA from Smoky Joe Wood, and he wasn't the most valuable player on the team. That honor belonged to Tris Speaker, who batted .383 with 53 doubles. Wood-Speaker in 1912 were the best one-two combination any team has ever had.

**2) Has there ever been another team that had two hitters like Ruth and Gehrig?**

Never, and no team is close. Ruth and Gehrig were by far the best hitters in the major leagues in 1927. One team has had the two most productive hitters on eight occasions:

| YEAR | HITTERS | TEAM |
|------|---------|------|
| 1880 | George Gorem, Abner Dalrymple | Chicago Cubs |
| 1884 | Charley Jones, John Reilly | Cincinnati Reds |
| 1927 | Babe Ruth, Lou Gehrig | New York Yankees |
| 1928 | Babe Ruth, Lou Gehrig | New York Yankees |
| 1930 | Babe Ruth, Lou Gehrig | New York Yankees |
| 1931 | Babe Ruth, Lou Gehrig | New York Yankees |
| 1959 | Hank Aaron, Eddie Mathews | Milwaukee Braves |
| 1989 | Will Clark, Kevin Mitchell | San Francisco Giants |

Of those other seven cases, the only ones that approach Ruth-Gehrig in 1927 are the other Ruth-Gehrig combinations. Think of it this way: Ruth and Gehrig batting third and fourth would be like a team today having Barry Bonds and Sammy Sosa batting third and fourth.

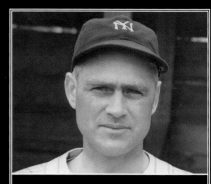

# EARLE COMBS
## Center Fielder

Combs, the Yankees center fielder during the Babe Ruth era, was a left-handed leadoff hitter who slapped the ball to all fields, was a skillful bunter, and ran exceptionally well. He was adept at fielding his position, but didn't have much of an arm. Combs, a career .325 hitter, generally was regarded as the best leadoff hitter of his era. He is in the Hall of Fame.

# WAITE HOYT
## Pitcher

Hoyt reached the majors as a teenager and stayed as a player and then a broadcaster for almost 60 years. He learned to pitch in Boston, where he was a teammate of Babe Ruth's, then joined Ruth and the Yankees in 1921. Hoyt took a regular turn in the Yankees rotation and won 17 to 20 games a year like clockwork through most of the 1920s. His most famous quote is: "The secret of success in pitching lies in getting a job with the Yankees." Hoyt is in the Hall of Fame.

**3) Did the 1927 Yankees have the greatest offense ever?**

Probably not. It depends on whether you mean the Yankees of 1927 specifically, or the Yankees of that era. If you mean the 1927 team, the answer is no. The 1931 and 1932 Yankees offenses were every bit as good, probably a little better, and other teams have had offenses just as good, including the 1975 and 1976 Cincinnati Reds, and the 1982 Milwaukee Brewers (Harvey's Wallbangers). If you mean the Yankees of that era, yes, it was the greatest offense ever put together.

**4) How good was the pitching staff?**

It was the best staff in the major leagues in 1927 because it was the deepest staff and the only one that had an effective relief ace. However, it is not among the 100 best staffs of all time. The four starters — Waite Hoyt, Herb Pennock, Urban Shocker and Dutch Ruether — had been around for years and knew how to pitch, but none was a Randy Johnson. The ace reliever, Wilcy Moore, had a good sinker and a deceptive motion, and turned in, by far, his best season.

**5) How good was the defense?**

It was spotty. Gehrig was okay, but not Gold Glove caliber. Tony Lazzeri was a decent second baseman by the standards of the time. Shortstop Mark Koenig had a fantastic arm but was an erratic fielder. Third baseman Joe Dugan had sure hands but had lost a step. Center fielder Earle Combs had very good range but couldn't throw. Ruth in right field and Bob Meusel in left had terrific arms but not a lot of speed. All of the other great Yankees teams were better defensively than the 1927 team.

**6) How many of the 1927 Yankees were the best players in the league at their position?**

Five: Gehrig, Ruth, Lazzeri, Combs and Moore. One National League center fielder, Hack Wilson, was as good as Combs that season, but no better. Two NL second basemen, Rogers Hornsby and Frankie Frisch, had better seasons than Lazzeri did. Koenig was the second-best shortstop in the league, and Meusel the third- or fourth-best left fielder. The other two regulars, Dugan and catcher Pat Collins, were about average. Moore had the best season ever by a reliever up to that point.

**7) Setting aside Ruth and Gehrig, how good was this team?**

If the 1927 Yankees had a .240 hitter without power instead of Ruth, it still is likely they would have won the pennant. If they had the worst first baseman in the league instead of Gehrig, they likely still would have won.

If they had neither Gehrig nor Ruth and been unable to replace them with quality players, the 1927 Yankees probably still would have had a record better than .500 and finished in third or fourth place.

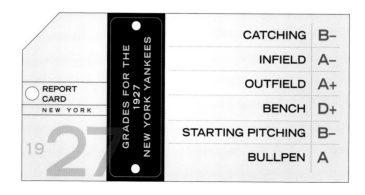

| REPORT CARD NEW YORK — GRADES FOR THE 1927 NEW YORK YANKEES | |
| --- | --- |
| CATCHING | B- |
| INFIELD | A- |
| OUTFIELD | A+ |
| BENCH | D+ |
| STARTING PITCHING | B- |
| BULLPEN | A |

# 1939

For fans of that era, the dominant story of the 1939 Yankees was the illness and retirement of Lou Gehrig. Yes, the team had a 106-45 record, won the pennant by 17 games, and won the World Series in four games — but the Yankees had won the pennant in each of the previous three years by an average of 14 games and had won all three World Series with comparative ease. It would have seemed strange to everyone at the time to have marked 1939 as one of the Yankees' greatest seasons, given the pall that hung over the season.

Years later, after the publication of baseball encyclopedias, after people began to try to organize baseball history, the case for the 1939 Yankees began to gather steam. Rob Neyer and Eddie Epstein wrote a book, *Baseball Dynasties*, in which they carefully weighed and measured the top candidates and concluded that the 1939 Yankees were the greatest team ever. And Richard J. Tofel wrote an excellent book just about the 1939 Yankees, *A Legend in the Making*.

With all due respect to Mr. Tofel's title, the 1939 Yankees are not defined by legend, but by logic. They have — or had for many years — very little legend, but awfully good credentials. They averaged more runs a game than the 1927 Yankees and yielded fewer — the 1927 Yankees led in runs, 975 to 967, but played three more games than the 1939 Yankees.

| THE REGULARS | | G | R | H | HR | RBI | BA | OBP |
|---|---|---|---|---|---|---|---|---|
| C | Bill Dickey | 128 | 98 | 145 | 24 | 105 | .302 | .403 |
| 1B | Babe Dahlgren | 144 | 71 | 125 | 15 | 89 | .235 | .312 |
| 2B | Joe Gordon | 151 | 92 | 161 | 28 | 111 | .284 | .370 |
| 3B | Red Rolfe | 152 | 139 | 213 | 14 | 80 | .329 | .404 |
| SS | Frank Crosetti | 152 | 109 | 153 | 10 | 56 | .233 | .315 |
| OF | George Selkirk | 128 | 103 | 128 | 21 | 101 | .306 | .452 |
| OF | Joe DiMaggio | 120 | 108 | 176 | 30 | 126 | .381 | .448 |
| OF | Charlie Keller | 111 | 87 | 133 | 11 | 83 | .334 | .447 |
| C | Tommy Henrich | 99 | 64 | 96 | 9 | 57 | .277 | .371 |
| Team | | 152 | 967 | 1,521 | 166 | 903 | .287 | .370 |
| AL rank | | | 1 | 2 | 1 | 1 | 2 | 1 |

| THE ROTATION | G | ERA | W | L | SV | IP | SO |
|---|---|---|---|---|---|---|---|
| Red Ruffing | 28 | 2.93 | 21 | 7 | 0 | 233 | 95 |
| Donald Atley | 24 | 3.71 | 13 | 3 | 1 | 153 | 55 |
| Bump Hadley | 26 | 2.98 | 12 | 6 | 2 | 154 | 65 |
| Lefty Gomez | 26 | 3.41 | 12 | 8 | 0 | 198 | 102 |
| Monte Pearson | 22 | 4.49 | 12 | 5 | 0 | 146 | 76 |
| Oral Hildebrand | 21 | 3.06 | 10 | 4 | 2 | 127 | 50 |
| Marius Russo | 21 | 2.41 | 8 | 3 | 2 | 116 | 55 |

| THE TOP RELIEVERS | | | | | | | |
|---|---|---|---|---|---|---|---|
| Johnny Murphy | 38 | 4.40 | 3 | 6 | 19 | 61 | 30 |
| Steve Sundra | 24 | 2.76 | 11 | 1 | 0 | 121 | 27 |
| Team | 152 | 3.31 | 106 | 45 | 26 | 1,349 | 565 |
| AL rank | | 1 | 1 | 1 | 1 | 7 | 3 |

The success of the 1927 Yankees rested heavily on the exploits of Lou Gehrig and Babe Ruth, while the 1939 team drew from a much broader base of support.

COMPARISON OF THE 1927 AND THE 1939 TEAMS, POSITION BY POSITION

| | 1927 | 1939 | COMMENT |
|---|---|---|---|
| C | Pat Collins | Bill Dickey | big edge 1939 |
| 1B | Lou Gehrig | Babe Dahlgren | huge edge 1927 |
| 2B | Tony Lazzeri | Joe Gordon | basically even |
| 3B | Joe Dugan | Red Rolfe | big edge 1939 |
| SS | Mark Koenig | Frank Crosetti | slim edge 1939 |
| LF | Bob Meusel | George Selkirk | about even |
| CF | Earle Combs | Joe DiMaggio | big edge 1939 |
| RF | Babe Ruth | Charlie Keller/ Tommy Henrich | you guess |

The 1939 team had the advantage at five of eight positions, and the teams had comparable pitching. The 1939 Yankees had the best catcher in the major leagues (Bill Dickey), the best second baseman (Joe Gordon), the best third baseman (Red Rolfe), and the best player in baseball in center field (Joe DiMaggio), plus a good shortstop, and three extremely productive players (Selkirk, Keller and Henrich) filling out the outfield.

Another standard of greatness: a team's accomplishments over a period of years. The Yankees won pennants in 1926, 1927, and 1928, and two World Series. Starting in 1936, the Yankees won four consecutive pennants, four consecutive World Championships, and seven pennants in eight seasons.

Another, more subtle argument on behalf of the 1939 team: Baseball matured significantly between 1927 and 1939. If you liken baseball history to a life cycle, the baseball of the 19th Century may be seen as an infant, and the dead-ball era (1901 to 1919) may be viewed as baseball's adolescence. The game in 1915 was loosely organized. Efforts to identify the best players and get them into the major leagues were haphazard at best. Players often reached the major leagues for no apparent reason other than that someone liked them, while more-skilled players remained in the minor leagues simply because the system to recognize and promote talent was in its rudimentary stage. This was less the case by 1927, but still true. Baseball in 1927 can be likened to a 21-year-old player — grown up but green as a ball field —

# JOE GORDON Second Baseman

Gordon was an acrobatic second baseman and a power hitter — a rare combination for a player at his position in the 1940s. He replaced Tony Lazzeri in 1938 and was virtually the same player as Lazzeri, although Lazzeri was not as smooth as Gordon in the field. Gordon averaged 25 homers and 100 RBI in his first five seasons, and he won the American League Most Valuable Player Award in 1942, getting more votes than Ted Williams, who had led the league in batting, home runs and RBI.

| REPORT CARD | GRADES FOR THE 1939 NEW YORK YANKEES | | |
|---|---|---|---|
| NEW YORK | | CATCHING | A |
| | | INFIELD | B+ |
| | | OUTFIELD | A+ |
| | | BENCH | C |
| | | STARTING PITCHING | C+ |
| | | BULLPEN | A+ |

*Charlie Keller, Joe DiMaggio and George Selkirk (left to right) carried big bats for the 1939 Yankees.*

while baseball in 1939 was much more mature. The Yankees in 1927 dominated an immature game with talent they had purchased from other teams. By 1939 they had a highly organized scouting and development operation that produced ballplayers.

Yet baseball cannot be viewed as a fully mature game until it admitted African-Americans in 1947, or maybe not until a few years after that. While the Yankees had a sophisticated farm system by 1939, some of the teams had nothing of the kind.

If you put the 1939 Yankees and the 1927 Yankees in a pennant race, the 1939 team probably would win.

One of the questions to ask about a great team is: What makes this team special? If you ask that question about the 1927 Yankees, you have an answer: They had the greatest one-two punch in baseball history and exceptional hitters surround-

ing them. It is also very easy to get an answer, if you ask that question about the 1961 Yankees, the 1998 Yankees, the 1911 Philadelphia Athletics or the 1974 Oakland A's. But it is not so easy to answer that question about the 1939 Yankees. What made that team special? A cold, mechanical efficiency? A farm system that was ahead of everyone else's? An exceptional ratio of runs scored to runs allowed? Those aren't very satisfactory answers, are they?

The 1939 Yankees were not greater than the 1927 Yankees — they were technically superior. The 1939 Yankees coped with and overcame tragedy. Maybe that should have elevated them to the status of legend — but the reality is, it didn't. Gehrig spent his life in the shadow of Babe Ruth. And perhaps the greatest team that Gehrig was part of was obscured for a long time by the shadow of his illness.

# 1961

In the spring of 1961, it was like baseball was reborn. Casey Stengel, manager of the Yankees seemingly forever, had been fired. His undoing came the previous fall, in the wonderful and exciting 1960 World Series that ended with Bill Mazeroski's home run. And the American League had expanded, for the first time ever, from eight to 10 teams.

B aseball still was the national game in 1961; football didn't explode in popularity until about three years later. Also, baseball fans had yet to develop the suspicion that club owners were ruining the game. That notion was hatched in 1969, when baseball split its leagues into divisions, and mushroomed in the 1970s, with the coming of the designated hitter and free agency. When AL expansion was announced in late 1960, a lot of people liked the idea, and probably just as many didn't — but there wasn't the "Oh, God, they're ruining the game again" reaction that tends to follow every change nowadays.

Baseball never went to sleep in the winter between the 1960 and 1961 seasons. A constant rumble echoed through the snow-covered months as discussion persisted about expansion and how it would affect the game. The 1961 season opened to an almost unparalleled level of interest.

The Yankees began the post-Stengel era by undoing a lot of what he had instituted. New manager Ralph Houk went from a five-man to a four-man pitching rotation, which gave Whitey Ford 10 more starts than in 1960 and enabled him to win 25

games. Houk also drastically scaled back Stengel's practice of platooning. Six Yankees got at least 500 at-bats in 1961; in the 12 Stengel years, only 33 players got 500 at-bats in a season.

The 1927, 1939 and 1998 Yankees led the league in runs scored and in fewest runs allowed, as did several other Yankees teams. The 1961 Yankees didn't lead the league in either category. They didn't lead in runs scored because, while they had phenomenal power, they had nothing except power. They didn't hit for a high average, didn't draw a lot of walks, didn't have a lot of speed, and didn't manufacture runs. Their power was awesome, but their leadoff hitters were mediocre. It was a Mark McGwire offense: nothing except home runs.

The Yankees went 109-53, won the pennant by eight games — Detroit, with hugely productive years from Norm Cash and Rocky Colavito, won 101 games — and beat the Reds in the World Series in five games. Yet we need to take into account that it was an expansion year, and that the 1961 Reds were perhaps the weakest champions in National League history.

The Yankees pitching staff didn't lead the

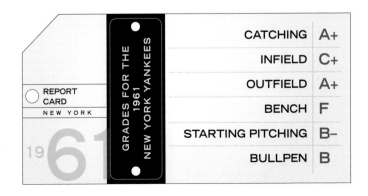

| REPORT CARD  NEW YORK | GRADES FOR THE 1961 NEW YORK YANKEES | CATCHING | A+ |
| | | INFIELD | C+ |
| | | OUTFIELD | A+ |
| | | BENCH | F |
| | | STARTING PITCHING | B− |
| | | BULLPEN | B |

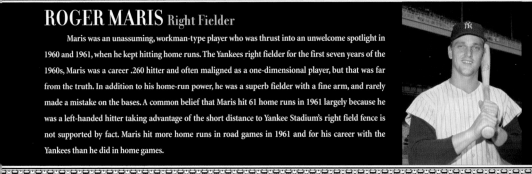

# ROGER MARIS Right Fielder

Maris was an unassuming, workman-type player who was thrust into an unwelcome spotlight in 1960 and 1961, when he kept hitting home runs. The Yankees right fielder for the first seven years of the 1960s, Maris was a career .260 hitter and often maligned as a one-dimensional player, but that was far from the truth. In addition to his home-run power, he was a superb fielder with a fine arm, and rarely made a mistake on the bases. A common belief that Maris hit 61 home runs in 1961 largely because he was a left-handed hitter taking advantage of the short distance to Yankee Stadium's right field fence is not supported by fact. Maris hit more home runs in road games in 1961 and for his career with the Yankees than he did in home games.

league in ERA because they had only about three good pitchers: Ford and Ralph Terry in the rotation, and Luis Arroyo in the bullpen. The rest of the staff was composed of kids who were good enough to win under the circumstances, those circumstances including a superb defense.

The 1961 Yankees catching corps — Elston Howard and Johnny Blanchard, and Yogi Berra for 15 games — was the best in major league history. Howard batting .348, backed by Blanchard hitting 21 homers, backed by Berra — that's better than Johnny Bench backed by Pat Corrales, Roy Campanella backed by Rube Walker, or any other combination you can name.

The 1961 Yankees bench gets a failing grade because:

1) It is among the weakest benches in history, even if you count Blanchard as part of the bench.

2) If you don't count Blanchard as part of the bench, it contributed virtually nothing.

The underrated part of the 1961 Yankees was the defense. The infield — Bill Skowron, Bobby Richardson, Tony Kubek and Clete Boyer — was phenomenal, all Gold Glove quality. Yet as hitters they had a combined on-base percentage of .306, about 20 points below what is marginally acceptable.

Four Yankees were the best in the major leagues at their positions in 1961: Howard, Arroyo (15-5, 29 saves), Roger Maris in right field and Mickey Mantle in center. Ford and Kubek, while not clearly better than their competitors, were as good as anyone at their positions. At the other positions, the 1961 Yankees were more or less an average team.

*(left to right) Moose Skowron, Roger Maris, Bobby Richardson, Elston Howard, Mickey Mantle*

If you put the 1961 Yankees in a pennant race with other great teams in history, they probably would get buried. In an eight-team league with the 1927 Yankees, 1939 Yankees, 1978 Yankees, 1998 Yankees, 1953 Dodgers, 1975 Reds, and 1970 Orioles, the 1961 Yankees would finish last. But there are other tests of greatness for a team: What did it accomplish over a period of years? In post-season play? Answer: A lot. The Yankees of this era won five straight pennants, and in both 1961 and 1963 won more than 100 games. The five-year run included two World Championships.

If we ask, What makes this team special? We get a clear answer: Power. The 1961 Yankees hit 240 home runs, a major league record that was not broken until 1996. Maris hit 61, a record that stood for 37 years. Maris and Mantle combined for 115, the most ever by two teammates. There was a lot of history in the making. The 1961 team, flawed as it might have been, was among the best in Yankees history.

## 1961 ROSTER

### THE REGULARS

|     |                 | G   | R   | H     | HR  | RBI | BA   | OBP  |
|-----|-----------------|-----|-----|-------|-----|-----|------|------|
| C   | Elston Howard   | 129 | 64  | 155   | 21  | 77  | .348 | .387 |
| 1B  | Bill Skowron    | 150 | 76  | 150   | 28  | 89  | .267 | .318 |
| 2B  | Bobby Richardson| 162 | 80  | 173   | 3   | 49  | .261 | .295 |
| 3B  | Clete Boyer     | 148 | 61  | 113   | 11  | 55  | .224 | .308 |
| SS  | Tony Kubek      | 153 | 84  | 170   | 8   | 46  | .276 | .306 |
| OF  | Roger Maris     | 161 | 132 | 159   | 61  | 142 | .269 | .372 |
| OF  | Mickey Mantle   | 153 | 132 | 163   | 54  | 128 | .317 | .448 |
| OF  | Yogi Berra      | 119 | 62  | 107   | 22  | 61  | .271 | .330 |
| C   | John Blanchard  | 93  | 38  | 74    | 21  | 54  | .305 | .382 |
| IF  | Hector Lopez    | 93  | 27  | 54    | 3   | 22  | .222 | .292 |
| C   | Bob Cerv        | 57  | 17  | 32    | 6   | 20  | .271 | .344 |
|     | Team            | 163 | 827 | 1,461 | 240 | 782 | .263 | .328 |
|     | AL rank         |     | 2   | 4     | 1   | 1   | 4    | 5    |

### THE ROTATION

|                 | G   | ERA  | W   | L   | SV  | IP    | SO  |
|-----------------|-----|------|-----|-----|-----|-------|-----|
| Whitey Ford     | 39  | 3.21 | 25  | 4   | 0   | 283   | 209 |
| Ralph Terry     | 31  | 3.15 | 16  | 3   | 0   | 188   | 86  |
| Bill Stafford   | 36  | 2.68 | 14  | 9   | 2   | 195   | 101 |
| Rollie Sheldon  | 35  | 3.60 | 11  | 5   | 0   | 163   | 84  |
| Bud Daley       | 23  | 3.96 | 8   | 9   | 0   | 130   | 83  |

### THE TOP RELIEVERS

|              | G   | ERA  | W   | L   | SV  | IP    | SO  |
|--------------|-----|------|-----|-----|-----|-------|-----|
| Luis Arroyo  | 65  | 2.19 | 15  | 5   | 29  | 119   | 87  |
| Jim Coates   | 43  | 3.44 | 11  | 5   | 5   | 141   | 80  |
| Team         | 163 | 3.46 | 109 | 53  | 39  | 1,451 | 866 |
| AL rank      |     | 2    | 1   |     | 1   | 3     | 4   |

### THE REGULARS

|    |                  | G   | R   | H     | HR  | RBI | BA   | OBP  |
|----|------------------|-----|-----|-------|-----|-----|------|------|
| C  | Thurman Munson   | 154 | 73  | 183   | 6   | 71  | .297 | .332 |
| 1B | Chris Chambliss  | 162 | 81  | 171   | 12  | 90  | .274 | .321 |
| 2B | Willie Randolph  | 134 | 87  | 139   | 3   | 42  | .279 | .381 |
| 3B | Graig Nettles    | 159 | 81  | 162   | 27  | 93  | .276 | .343 |
| SS | Bucky Dent       | 123 | 40  | 92    | 5   | 40  | .243 | .286 |
| OF | Mickey Rivers    | 141 | 78  | 148   | 11  | 48  | .265 | .302 |
| OF | Reggie Jackson   | 139 | 82  | 140   | 27  | 97  | .274 | .356 |
| OF | Lou Piniella     | 130 | 67  | 148   | 6   | 69  | .314 | .361 |
| DH | Cliff Johnson    | 76  | 20  | 32    | 6   | 19  | .184 | .307 |
| OF | Roy White        | 103 | 44  | 93    | 8   | 43  | .269 | .349 |
| SS | Fred Stanley     | 81  | 14  | 35    | 1   | 9   | .219 | .324 |
|    | Team             | 163 | 735 | 1,489 | 125 | 693 | .267 | .328 |
|    | AL rank          |     | 4   | 4     | 6   | 4   | 4    | 7    |

### THE ROTATION

|                | G   | ERA  | W   | L   | SV  | IP    | SO  |
|----------------|-----|------|-----|-----|-----|-------|-----|
| Ron Guidry     | 35  | 1.74 | 25  | 3   | 0   | 274   | 248 |
| Ed Figueroa    | 35  | 2.99 | 20  | 9   | 0   | 253   | 92  |
| Catfish Hunter | 21  | 3.58 | 12  | 6   | 0   | 118   | 56  |
| Dick Tidrow    | 31  | 3.84 | 7   | 11  | 0   | 185   | 73  |
| Jim Beattie    | 25  | 3.73 | 6   | 9   | 0   | 128   | 65  |

### THE TOP RELIEVERS

| Rich Gossage   | 63  | 2.01 | 10  | 11  | 27  | 134   | 122 |
|----------------|-----|------|-----|-----|-----|-------|-----|
| Sparky Lyle    | 59  | 3.47 | 9   | 3   | 9   | 112   | 33  |
| Ken Clay       | 28  | 4.28 | 3   | 4   | 0   | 76    | 32  |
| Team           | 163 | 3.18 | 100 | 63  | 36  | 1,460 | 817 |
| AL rank        |     | 1    | 1   | 1   | 1   | 2     | 2   |

# 1978

From 1921 through 1964, the longest the Yankees went without winning the American League pennant was three years. In those 44 years the team had a losing record only once (69-85 in 1925), finished 20 games out of first place only once (in 1925), and had a winning percentage of less than .600 only 13 times.

T hen came the dark period in Yankees history. From 1965 through 1975, the team had losing records five times, finished 20 games out of first place six times, and had a winning percentage as high as .550 only once. The Yankees of that era certainly were not as hapless as the Boston Braves of the 1920s or the San Diego Padres of the 1970s, yet they no longer were entertaining their fans in the manner to which those fans had become accustomed.

That changed for the better starting in 1976, when the Yankees won the first of three successive AL pennants. In 1977 they won the World Championship for the first time in 15 years, and a year later the team was even better, one of the best in Yankees history. The 1978 team went 100-63, including a dramatic win in Boston in a playoff for the AL East title, and beat the Los Angeles Dodgers in six games in the World Series.

The story of the 1978 Yankees, as it played out at the time, was the saga of a team winning its second successive World Championship despite a clubhouse rocked by dissension. In 1977 the big addition to the team was Reggie Jackson. He was

the straw that constantly stirred something. In 1978 the big addition was Goose Gossage, who was brought in to be the closer, even though the 1977 closer, Sparky Lyle, had performed so well that he won the AL Cy Young Award.

Jackson and Thurman Munson clearly resented each other, Lyle had a chip on his shoulder, and Cliff Johnson was a smoldering powder keg. The veterans Lou Piniella, Graig Nettles and Dick Tidrow, though not exactly controversial figures, were quick to speak up if they felt someone was stepping on their toes. And the man in the manager's seat, Billy Martin, was the most volatile personality in the clubhouse, at least until he resigned under pressure in late July and was replaced by the mellow Bob Lemon.

From the high ground of retrospect, it seems evident that the 1978 Yankees probably didn't have any more internal conflict than most teams. It just seemed that way because the Yankees were followed by a large press corps, and the sports media, in the wake of Watergate, had moved off a cooperative, go-along, and get-along approach and into a more aggressive mode. No doubt there was conflict among the 1958 Yankees and the 1928 Yankees, too; it just never made the newspapers, so the public was unaware of it.

The 1978 Yankees came together at the onset of the free-agent era. The great teams that preceded the 1978 Yankees largely were populated by players who went through the minor leagues together and had played together for years. The 1978 Yankees were a group of players thrown together in mid-career, veterans who were set in their ways and had to figure out how to get along to go along. "Clubhouse chemistry" is perhaps the most misunderstood term in sports. It doesn't mean that everyone likes each other and gets along famously. It means that a team has a lot of players that do not deal well with losing. This team had many of those guys — the type that wouldn't stand for losing, was miserable when it happened, and didn't care if he made everyone around him miserable, too.

How good were the 1978 Yankees? Let's con- sider their key players. Munson was the AL MVP in 1976, although he was not as good a player in 1978. Jackson was the AL MVP in 1973 and now is in the Hall of Fame. Lyle and Gossage were among the top closers of their era. Nettles at third base and Willie Randolph at second base were two of the best players the Yankees ever had at those positions. Ron Guidry went 25-3 and had a 1.74 ERA, the best season by a Yankees pitcher since Lefty Gomez went 26-5 with a 2.33 ERA in 1934.

No one element of the team, other than the bullpen, was truly outstanding. Every other factor of the team was very good — and that is quite unusual. Almost every team has a weakness.

What makes the 1978 Yankees special? Two things:

1) They succeeded through turmoil that played out daily in the news media.

2) They wrote the manual for success in the free-agent era.

## SPARKY LYLE Pitcher

Lyle's seven seasons with the Yankees were by far the best of his 16-year career. His achievement for the Yankees —141 saves, 57 victories — makes him the top left-handed reliever in club history and the third-best reliever overall, behind Mariano Rivera and Goose Gossage. Lyle's best season was in 1977, when he led the American League in appearances with 72, won 13 games and saved 26, had a 2.13 ERA, and became the first reliever to win the AL Cy Young Award. Lyle pitched 137 innings in 1977, a total that was exceeded only six times through the rest of the century by pitchers with at least 20 saves.

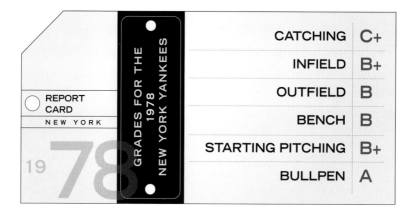

| | | |
|---|---|---|
| CATCHING | C+ |
| INFIELD | B+ |
| OUTFIELD | B |
| BENCH | B |
| STARTING PITCHING | B+ |
| BULLPEN | A |

REPORT CARD
NEW YORK

GRADES FOR THE 1978 NEW YORK YANKEES

19**78**

And perhaps there is a third reason: They had many stars. Jackson, Gossage, Munson, Nettles, Piniella, Randolph, Guidry, Chris Chambliss, Mickey Rivers — these guys were really good players. Tony Lazzeri played second base and Earle Combs center field for the 1927 Yankees, and both are in the Hall of Fame. Randolph was a better player than Lazzeri, and Rivers was much the same player as Combs, though not quite as good. Guidry was every bit as good as Herb Pennock, the star lefthander on the 1927 team. Continuing the matchup of the 1978 Yankees and the 1927 Yankees, Jackson certainly was not Babe Ruth and Chambliss was not Lou Gehrig, but Munson and Nettles were far better than Pat Collins and Joe Dugan. Virtually everyone in the 1978 lineup except shortstop Bucky Dent could be called a star — and he certainly lived at that level when his home run over the Green Monster in the playoff game beat the Red Sox and set in motion the Yankees' march to another World Championship.

# 1998

In the summer and fall of 1998, as the Yankees marched to 114 wins and decisive victories over three postseason opponents, many people asked: Is this the greatest team of all time? Where does this team rank among the best ever? Those questions could not be answered, since there was much about the 1998 Yankees that could not have been known in 1998. It takes time to understand what has happened.

Five years is not long enough for the whole truth to emerge, but it is sufficient to allow the drivel to drain off. Accordingly, it is not irresponsible to conclude after five years that the 1998 Yankees were the greatest baseball team of all time. Why? Let us begin with the question: What are the standards of a great team?

1) It should dominate its competition.

The 1998 Yankees won the American League East by 22 games and went 11-2 in three levels of postseason play. That is about as thoroughly as any team has ever dominated its competition.

2) It needs to be successful over a period of years.

This team won three successive World Series and four in five years in an era when winning the World Championship required three straight series conquests over high quality teams. No other team in history has accomplished that much in postseason play.

3) It should have — at the least — a good offense, good defense and good pitching staff.

The 1998 Yankees had an incredible offense, getting about 100 runs created from every position except left field. They had five good starting pitchers, backed up by five good relievers — an absolutely astonishing staff. Their defense, while not as strong as the other two elements, was competent.

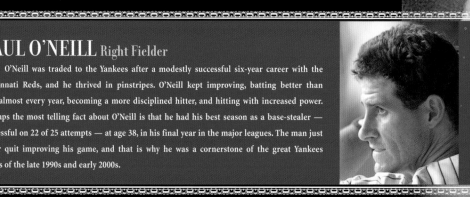

## PAUL O'NEILL Right Fielder

O'Neill was traded to the Yankees after a modestly successful six-year career with the Cincinnati Reds, and he thrived in pinstripes. O'Neill kept improving, batting better than .300 almost every year, becoming a more disciplined hitter, and hitting with increased power. Perhaps the most telling fact about O'Neill is that he had his best season as a base-stealer — successful on 22 of 25 attempts — at age 38, in his final year in the major leagues. The man just never quit improving his game, and that is why he was a cornerstone of the great Yankees teams of the late 1990s and early 2000s.

### THE REGULARS

| | | G | R | H | HR | RBI | BA | OBP |
|---|---|---|---|---|---|---|---|---|
| C | Jorge Posada | 111 | 56 | 96 | 17 | 63 | .268 | .350 |
| 1B | Tino Martinez | 142 | 92 | 149 | 28 | 123 | .281 | .355 |
| 2B | Chuck Knoblauch | 150 | 117 | 160 | 17 | 64 | .265 | .361 |
| 3B | Scott Brosius | 152 | 86 | 159 | 19 | 98 | .300 | .371 |
| SS | Derek Jeter | 149 | 127 | 203 | 19 | 84 | .324 | .384 |
| LF | Chad Curtis | 151 | 79 | 111 | 10 | 56 | .243 | .355 |
| CF | Bernie Williams | 128 | 101 | 169 | 26 | 97 | .339 | .422 |
| RF | Paul O'Neill | 152 | 95 | 191 | 24 | 116 | .317 | .372 |
| DH | Darryl Strawberry | 101 | 44 | 73 | 24 | 57 | .247 | .354 |
| OF | Tim Raines | 109 | 53 | 93 | 5 | 47 | .290 | .395 |
| C | Joe Girardi | 78 | 31 | 70 | 3 | 31 | .276 | .317 |
| Team | | 162 | 965 | 1,625 | 207 | 907 | .288 | .362 |
| AL rank | | | 1 | 2 | 4 | 1 | 2 | 1 |

### THE ROTATION

| | G | ERA | W | L | SV | IP | SO |
|---|---|---|---|---|---|---|---|
| David Cone | 31 | 3.55 | 20 | 7 | 0 | 208 | 209 |
| David Wells | 30 | 3.49 | 18 | 4 | 0 | 214 | 163 |
| Andy Pettitte | 33 | 4.24 | 16 | 11 | 0 | 216 | 146 |
| Hideki Irabu | 29 | 4.06 | 13 | 9 | 0 | 173 | 126 |
| Orlando Hernandez | 21 | 3.13 | 12 | 4 | 0 | 141 | 131 |

### THE TOP RELIEVERS

| | G | ERA | W | L | SV | IP | SO |
|---|---|---|---|---|---|---|---|
| Mariano Rivera | 54 | 1.91 | 3 | 0 | 36 | 61 | 36 |
| Graeme Lloyd | 50 | 1.67 | 3 | 0 | 0 | 38 | 20 |
| Ramiro Mendoza | 41 | 3.25 | 10 | 2 | 1 | 130 | 56 |
| Darren Holmes | 34 | 3.33 | 0 | 3 | 2 | 51 | 31 |
| Jeff Nelson | 45 | 3.79 | 5 | 3 | 3 | 40 | 35 |
| Mike Stanton | 67 | 5.47 | 4 | 1 | 6 | 79 | 69 |
| Team | 162 | 3.82 | 114 | 48 | 48 | 1,456 | 1,080 |
| AL rank | | 1 | 1 | 1 | 3 | 3 | 4 |

**4) It should have great players having great years.**

The 1998 Yankees do not score as well here as in the other areas. Derek Jeter and Bernie Williams both had outstanding seasons, and both could have Hall of Fame credentials by the end of their careers. Yet there was no Babe Ruth, no Joe DiMaggio, no Mickey Mantle on this team. The top three stars of the 1950s Yankees teams — Mantle, Yogi Berra, Whitey Ford — all would have ranked ahead of anyone on the 1998 team.

**5) It should be deep in truly talented players.**

A truly talented player is one who has had more than one good season. A truly great team is not composed of six guys having career years. On this standard, the 1998 Yankees rank far, far ahead of any other team in history. Of the 10 players on the team who had 300 or more plate appearances, nine could be considered truly talented. We have mentioned Jeter and Williams. Here are the others:

- Jorge Posada, who was having his first good season, has become one of the best catchers of his era.
- First baseman Tino Martinez, who drove in 123 runs, has had five other 100-RBI seasons.
- Second baseman Chuck Knoblauch scored 100 or more runs six times, and was in position to make a run at 3,000 hits until his fielding work betrayed him and his reputation collapsed along with his defense in 1999.
- Third baseman Scott Brosius, although he didn't hit as well the rest of his career as he did in 1998 (.300, 98 RBI) was a fine defensive player and had more than 1,000 hits in his career.
- Outfielder Tim Raines, who hit .290 with a .395 on-base percentage, was a Hall of Fame–caliber player over the course of his career, although the press never recognized it.
- Darryl Strawberry, who hit 24 homers as a half-time player in 1998, was a feared power hitter for many years.
- Right fielder Paul O'Neill hit .300 or better in each of his first six seasons with the Yankees, had at least 100 RBI in four successive seasons, and was a player who did everything well.

Literally every player the Yankees put on the field, except left fielder Chad Curtis, meets the standard of a player of substance. And Curtis, while he did not hit enough to be a high-quality outfielder, had more than 1,000 hits, more than 100 home runs, and more than 200 stolen bases in his career.

A few teams in history have had a stronger eight-man lineup than the 1998 Yankees, namely the 1953 Brooklyn Dodgers, the 1962 San Francisco Giants, the 1975 Cincinnati Reds and the 1976 Reds.

# YET NONE HAD THE DEPTH OF QUALITY ON THEIR PITCHING STAFF TO MATCH THAT OF THE 1998 YANKEES.

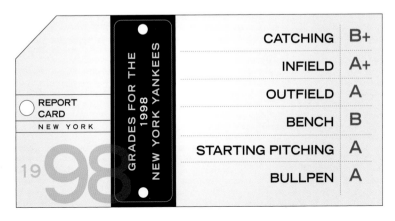

| REPORT CARD NEW YORK | GRADES FOR THE 1998 NEW YORK YANKEES | |
|---|---|---|
| | CATCHING | B+ |
| | INFIELD | A+ |
| | OUTFIELD | A |
| | BENCH | B |
| | STARTING PITCHING | A |
| | BULLPEN | A |

*Jorge Posada (left) and Derek Jeter (right).*

A few teams in history have had a stronger eight-man lineup than the 1998 Yankees, namely the 1953 Brooklyn Dodgers, the 1962 San Francisco Giants, the 1975 Cincinnati Reds, and the 1976 Reds. Yet none had the depth of quality on their pitching staff to match that of the 1998 Yankees. The top three starters that year — Andy Pettitte, David Wells and David Cone — have more than 500 victories among them. Orlando Hernandez, the fourth starter, has been a star for many years, although most were in Cuba. Relievers Mariano Rivera, Ramiro Mendoza, Mike Stanton, Jeff Nelson and Darren Holmes are genuinely fine pitchers, and there were others that were pretty effective.

No other team in baseball history has ever had as many truly talented players having good to great seasons as the 1998 Yankees.

The 1998 Yankees infield was far better than those of the four other great Yankees teams, but not the best in team history. Here are the top five infields in Yankees history (players are listed in order at first base, second base, third base and shortstop):

1) 2004 (Jason Giambi, Miguel Cairo, Alex Rodriguez, Derek Jeter)

2) 2002 (Jason Giambi, Alfonso Soriano, Robin Ventura, Derek Jeter)

3) 1936 (Lou Gehrig, Tony Lazzeri, Red Rolfe, Frankie Crosetti)

4) 1998 (Tino Martinez, Chuck Knoblauch, Scott Brosius, Derek Jeter)

5) 1932 (Lou Gehrig, Tony Lazzeri, Joe Sewell, Frankie Crosetti)

One test of a great team is its ability to thrive under any circumstances. Envision a Super League, in which the great teams of all time compete against one another. Could the 1998 Yankees travel to 1906 and compete against the Chicago Cubs in a dead-ball-era game? Could the 1998 Yankees travel to 1975 and compete against the Reds in Cincinnati on an artificial turf field where any ball that hit the ground was likely to scoot to the wall?

The answers lie in the completeness of the 1998 Yankees. They hit 207 home runs (a huge number), and also had a .288 batting average, 153 stolen bases in 216 attempts (an excellent success ratio), and 653 walks. With Jeter, Knoblauch, Williams, Curtis and Raines in the lineup, they could have stolen 250 bases easily if they had reason to do it. With quality right-handed and left-handed pitchers both in the rotation and the bullpen, excellent right-handed and left-handed hitters, power, speed, a high batting average and good defense, the 1998 Yankees could march into any city in any era and win more frequently than any of their opponents. That makes it the greatest team in baseball history.

| | YRS | W | L | PCT | WHAT THEY WON |
|---|---|---|---|---|---|
| **Miller Huggins** | | | | | |
| Yankees | 12 | 1,067 | 719 | .597 | 6 pennants, 3 World Championships |
| Other Teams | 5 | 346 | 415 | .455 | Nothing |
| **Joe McCarthy** | | | | | |
| Yankees | 16 | 1,460 | 867 | .627 | 8 pennants, 7 World Championships |
| Other Teams | 8 | 665 | 466 | .588 | 1 pennant |
| **Casey Stengel** | | | | | |
| Yankees | 12 | 1,149 | 696 | .623 | 10 pennants, 7 World Championships |
| Other Teams | 13 | 756 | 1,146 | .397 | Nothing |
| **Ralph Houk** | | | | | |
| Yankees | 11 | 944 | 806 | .539 | 3 pennants, 2 World Championships |
| Other Teams | 16 | 1,157 | 1,135 | .505 | Nothing |
| **Billy Martin** | | | | | |
| Yankees | 8 | 556 | 385 | .591 | 2 divisions, 2 pennants, 1 World Championship |
| Other Teams | 11 | 697 | 628 | .526 | 3 divisions |
| **Joe Torre** | | | | | |
| Yankees | 8 | 786 | 506 | .608 | 7 divisions, 6 pennants, 4 World Championships |
| Other Teams | 14 | 894 | 1,003 | .471 | 1 division |

# THE MANAGERS

Casey Stengel was one of the most popular managers in baseball history, but he was not the team's greatest manager. That honor goes to Joe McCarthy, who might well be the greatest manager ever from among all teams.

McCarthy's record is much better than Stengel's or Joe Torre's. McCarthy, Stengel and Torre managed other teams before the Yankees. McCarthy was tremendously successful before he joined the Yankees, tremendously successful with the Yankees, and he had a .604 winning percentage after he left the Yankees. Stengel, too, was very successful with the Yankees, but his teams never won more than 77 games in a season before he joined the Yankees, and he had a .302 winning percentage after he left the Yankees. Among the Yankees who played for both McCarthy and Stengel, most were asked many times to compare the two. Virtually all of them said McCarthy was the better manager.

However, two things should be noted:

1) Stengel's record, when he managed poor teams, has nothing to do with how well he managed the Yankees.

2) How good is a specific manager? The question cannot be answered objectively. Whether a manager's record is good or bad depends on the talent of his players and his ability to get the most out of them — a relationship that no one can really measure. Why waste time debating questions that have no objective answer? It is more worthwhile to try and understand how managers differ from one another; how they take different paths but try to get to the same place. The Yankees have had tremendously successful teams under five different managers — or six, if you count the Billy Martin/Bob Lemon/Gene Michael/Dick Howser shuffle, which we will label *Martin* for space considerations. The six, in the order of eras: Miller Huggins, McCarthy, Stengel, Ralph Houk, Martin and Joe Torre. Following are discussions of each man.

1) Huggins represented a type of manager — the scrappy, contentious former middle-infielder — that is so common now that one might assume it always has been the dominant model of a manager. In fact, it was uncommon in Huggins' era.

2) Huggins managed the Yankees during their successful conversion from an early John McGraw–style organization to a modern Branch Rickey–style organization.

Discussing the second point first, when Huggins was hired to manage the Yankees in 1918, teams did not have front offices, as they do now. The manager was more or less responsible for the composition of his team's roster, much as a college basketball coach is today. The manager personally signed and trained young players that he liked. Drawing on his network of acquaintances in the game and on a few scouts who reported to him, the manager made the decision to purchase players from minor league operations, and he made trades with other managers.

Thus, Huggins' success in his early seasons as a manager was based largely on his judgment of talent. He had an advantage in that the Yankees had owners who were willing and able to put money into a deal to get the players they wanted. But as we have seen many times, spending alone doesn't lead to success. Huggins recognized the type of player who could help him win, and in his early years as the Yankees manager he was the leading force in acquiring those players.

Within three years of Huggins becoming the Yankees manager, teams began to hire front office executives who took responsibility for acquiring talent, and scouts whose role it was to locate promising players and sign them. At the same time, teams

**MILLER HUGGINS**
1918–1929

began to form farm systems to feed talent to the major league team.

Huggins was the only manager to run his team successfully through this transition. John McGraw continued to run the New York Giants the old-school way until the end of his career in 1932, and Connie Mack tried to do everything himself until it became apparent that a one-man show just couldn't compete with the increasingly organized and sophisticated baseball operations. While many organizations were thrashing around trying to sort out this new relationship between manager and front office, Huggins backed off gracefully and allowed the Yankees to develop a state-of-the-art operation. Thus, to a certain extent the achievements of later Yankees teams can be traced back to Huggins.

As for the first point: Huggins as a player led the National League in walks four times, even though nobody was aware of it back then. At that time, a walk was considered a non-event for the batter. Huggins took all those walks not because he got paid for it, but because that was the type of player he was; he knew that getting on base helped the team win, and he did it, even though nobody was counting.

As a player with virtually no talent — he was slow as well as tiny — Huggins had to scrap for every edge he could find. He took the same mindset into managing. Huggins was detail-oriented, understood the game and why some teams won and others didn't.

The biggest, strongest, and loudest players tended to evolve into managers in the 1800s and through the first 25 years of the 20th Century. Huggins was a departure from the norm, a 135-pound second baseman who became a manager and succeeded on his wits.

1) McCarthy understood how an offense works better than any other manager in history.

2) McCarthy had great confidence in his ability to judge talent — and thus no fear of his players.

If you make a list of the highest-scoring teams in major league history between 1900 and 1996, McCarthy's teams dominate it. You think: Gehrig and Ruth, sure; they scored more runs than anyone else did. But of the four highest-scoring non-Yankees teams in that period, three were McCarthy's teams: the 1929 and 1930 Chicago Cubs, and the 1950 Boston Red Sox, who were built by McCarthy, although he resigned as manager in midseason.

McCarthy was virtually a genius at putting together an offense. Long before anyone else, he grasped the importance of hitters taking pitches and running long counts to put pressure on the pitcher. McCarthy understood something that isn't well understood today: A combination of little guys who punch the ball and try to get on base and big guys who look for a pitch they can drive to the moon is much more effective than either type

JOE McCARTHY
1931–1946

by itself. Today, we have phenomenal individual batting numbers, and we also have some teams on which everyone tries to be a home run hitter. McCarthy realized that it's a lot easier to get a single, a walk, and a homer than it is to get three solo homers. That was true then, and it is true now.

A book written a few years ago included a passage about how McCarthy did not like to use rookies. This is historical ignorance on the same scale as saying that Tony La Russa does not like left-handed relievers. McCarthy had no trepidation about putting a rookie into the starting lineup or into the rotation, and thus no fear of telling veteran players

exactly what he expected them to do and exactly how he expected them to do it. In that regard, he was unique among managers of his time.

McCarthy played and managed in the minor leagues, but he never played in the major leagues. His view of the baseball world — accurate at that time — was that there were a lot of guys in the minor leagues who were every bit as good as the guys in the majors. McCarthy believed a major league manager needed to establish good rapport with players of exceptional ability, but otherwise the talent was fungible. If a lesser player didn't want to go along with the manager's program, to hell with him, there were many who could take his place.

One more point on McCarthy: He was the first to divide a pitching staff into starters and relievers. At the onset of baseball history, there were only starters. By 1925 a fair percentage of games involved the use of relief pitchers, but there really was no such thing as a pure starter or a pure reliever. Literally every pitcher in the 1925 to 1935 era was used both as a starter and a reliever, as the occasion demanded. McCarthy in 1936 gave his pitchers definitive roles in the rotation or in the bullpen. The Yankees won four straight pennants, and the idea caught on.

————

1) Stengel was ahead of his time in the use of his bench.

2) The sources of advantage for Stengel's teams were double plays and home runs.

When professional baseball was first played, it was dominated by a few exceptional athletes. Teams attempted to gather as many of those athletes as possible and filled the rest of the roster in ad hoc fashion. As the game became popular, the talent base grew and became better trained, and the difference between the best players and those at the bottom of the roster narrowed dramatically. Stengel was among the first managers to recognize this and use it to his team's advantage. By platooning, by revising his lineup daily, Stengel got 200, 300, even 400 at-bats a year for his bench players — in a time when many managers were perfectly content to write out a lineup in April and ride it through September.

A statistical measure called Bench Value Percentage shows how well Stengel used his reserve players. In Stengel's first season as a manager, his 1934 Brooklyn Dodgers had the highest Bench Value Percentage in the major leagues. They led again in 1935 and were third in 1936. Stengel's 1940 and 1941 Boston Braves each had the highest Bench Value Percentage in the majors. With the Yankees, he had the highest percentage in the majors in 1949, 1951, and 1954. Even with the awful New York Mets in 1962 and 1963, he had the highest Bench Value Percentage in the major leagues. When Stengel's teams didn't lead in this category, they were close to the top.

**CASEY STENGEL**
1949–1960

When Stengel managed poor teams, this didn't help him at all. But when he managed the Yankees and had a regular and predictable flow of talent, it helped him a lot. Most managers commit themselves to certain players and are reluctant to make changes. If a second baseman has a good season, almost any manager will pencil that second baseman into his lineup the next season and stick with him. Not Stengel. His second baseman was Jerry Coleman one year, Billy Martin the next, Gil McDougald the year after that, then Martin again, then Jerry Lumpe, then Bobby Richardson. It

wasn't that these guys were not good players. But if one was in a slump, he had about a week to get his bat going before Stengel turned to someone else.

On a bad team, this chronic impatience can be destructive. How can you develop a talent core with an impatient manager? But on a good team, it works well. Stengel didn't allow a second baseman to play 150 games and hit .232 with 4 homers and 38 RBI. He recognized the strengths and weaknesses of his players and used them accordingly. Stengel liked to rotate four or five outfielders, giving each 350 to 450 at-bats. If one stopped hitting and dropped out of the rotation, someone else went into the slot. And it was usually a good player, because the Yankees had more good players than any other team in those days.

Concerning the second point, Stengel's Yankees teams had huge advantages over their opponents in only two areas: double plays and home runs. In 1948, the year before Stengel became manager, the Yankees turned 161 double plays and their hitters grounded into 136. In 1949 the double plays increased to 195, and the hitters grounded into 141. That's a plus 54; the league average was plus 39. In 1950 the Yankees were plus 66, by 1952 they were plus 106, in 1954 they were plus 104, and in 1956 plus 112. You might imagine that these advantages are common for a good team — but they are not. Good teams have more runners on base than their opponents do, thus they often have little or no advantage in double plays.

Stengel worked at maximizing his team's double play advantage. He tried to avoid putting two right-handed sluggers back-to-back in the lineup because that type of hitter is susceptible to the double play. He preferred ground-ball pitchers,

# The Wisdom of
# CASEY STENGEL

* "Been in this game 100 years, but I see new ways to lose 'em I never knew existed before."

* "Being with a woman all night never hurt no professional baseball player. It's staying up all night looking for a woman that does him in."

* "Good pitching will always stop good hitting and vice versa."

* "Yogi Berra could fall in a sewer and come up with a gold watch."

* "Mickey Mantle has it in his body to be great."

* "I couldna done it without my players."

* "I feel greatly honored to have a ballpark named after me, especially since I've been thrown out of so many."

* "If we're going to win the pennant, we've got to start thinking we're not as good as we think we are."

* "I got players with bad watches; they can't tell midnight from noon."

* "It's wonderful to meet so many friends that I didn't used to like."

* "Managing is getting paid for home runs someone else hits."

* "Son, we'd like to keep you around this season, but we're going to try and win a pennant."

* "The secret of managing is to keep the guys who hate you away from the guys who are undecided."

* "The Yankees don't pay me to win every day, just two out of three."

* "They say some of my stars drink whiskey, but I have found that ones who drink milkshakes don't win many ball games."

* "They told me my services were no longer desired because they wanted to put in a youth program as an advance way of keeping the club going. I'll never make the mistake of being 70 again."

* "You have to go broke three times to learn how to make a living."

and he liked hitters who put the ball in the air; one induced double plays, the other avoided them. The primary reasons the Yankees traded for Roger Maris in December 1959 were that Maris batted left-handed and hit the ball in the air. He batted only .240 in 1958, but hit 28 homers and grounded into only two double plays — Stengel's type of player.

⬥

The Yankees in their first three seasons under Houk won 309 games and two World Championships. He succeeded essentially for two reasons:

1) He worked exceptionally well with young pitchers.

2) He wasn't Casey Stengel.

Houk in his first three years as Yankees manager put Bill Stafford, Rollie Sheldon, Jim Bouton, and Al Downing in the rotation, and all were effective starters for a while. Every spring Houk surveyed the young pitchers in his camp, found a couple who weren't far away, simplified and focused their approach to pitching, and put them in the rotation. Talented 22- and 23-year-old kids who go into a rotation usually pitch well for a year or two, then hurt their arms. But for the short run, this strategy works fine if you have good kids to work with and know how to teach them, and that certainly was the case with the Yankees and Houk, who had been a backup catcher in his playing career.

After 12 years under Stengel, the Yankees were ready for a change in 1961, and Houk got the job. Probably no one was more grateful than Whitey Ford. Stengel, at the suggestion of pitching coach Jim Turner, used a five-man rotation 20 years before

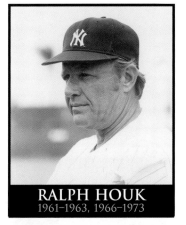

**RALPH HOUK**
1961–1963, 1966–1973

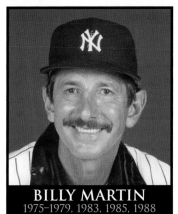

**BILLY MARTIN**
1975–1979, 1983, 1985, 1988

anyone else did. Stengel not only used a five-man rotation, but also held back pitchers to get more favorable matchups. Stengel almost never used Ford in Boston, for example, and, if the Yankees were playing the Senators and then the Indians, he would hold back Ford to pitch against the Indians, figuring the Yankees probably could beat the Senators with Duke Maas or the like. While this strategy was effective, it limited Ford to 25 to 29 starts a year. Houk went to a four-man rotation and it paid off quickly for Ford, who got 39 starts in 1961 and went 25-4.

Houk also scaled back considerably Stengel's practice of platooning, which certainly placated those chosen to play regularly. In 1961 second baseman Bobby Richardson and third baseman Clete Boyer each got more than 500 at-bats for the first time and proved to be championship-caliber players.

⬥

So much has been written about Martin that it is difficult to offer original observations, or even trite ones that can be disguised as original. However, with respect to Martin's well-known affection for Casey Stengel, we can note these two points:

1) Martin was very much like Stengel as an offensive manager.

2) Martin was very different from Stengel as a defensive manager.

Martin had many bench players — like Oscar Gamble, Jim Spencer and Fred Stanley — who were typical of Stengel's bench players. All had limitations as regulars, but were very productive in well-defined roles. Like Stengel, Martin did not have a lot of patience with players who stopped producing.

Martin also learned from Stengel the value of players who didn't hit into a lot of double plays. Martin liked left-handed hitters who hit the ball in the air. The players he had who hit the ball on the ground were mostly quick enough to stay out of double plays, like Mickey Rivers and Willie Randolph. Martin compensated for a right-handed hitter who was a threat to hit into a double play, like Bucky Dent, by often calling for a bunt or having base-runners moving with the pitch.

Unlike Stengel's teams, Martin's teams did not turn a lot of double plays. Martin did not focus on procuring ground-ball pitchers, as Stengel did. And whereas Stengel's ideal pitching staff was eight starters, five of whom could also work in relief, Martin's ideal staff was four guys who could pitch 325 innings each. Like Ralph Houk had done, Martin in his own way reacted against his mentor, doing some things the exact opposite of how Stengel did.

**JOE TORRE**
1996-PRESENT

It seems that the parallels between Torre and Casey Stengel are both broad and profound. Both began their managerial careers with poor New York teams in the National League, and both had managed several National League teams with limited success before getting to the Yankees. The Yankees hired both when they were at a relatively advanced age, in their late 50s, and each launched the Yankees into a series of enormously successful seasons.

Their personalities could not have been more different — Stengel was a clown; Torre is a reflective, mature leader — yet each became a master at dealing with the New York media, a challenge that many a manager hasn't met successfully.

Like Stengel, Torre has been successful with the Yankees because his managerial style works better with a good team than with a poor team. Like Stengel, Torre likes to use a lot of pitchers; if he opened spring training with 14 proven pitchers, Torre would be looking for a 15th. When a manager has scarce resources, he should determine his three best pitchers and figure out how to get the most from them. But with a team that can bring in the likes of Dwight Gooden or Orlando Hernandez and add him to an already well-stocked staff, Torre's style is well-suited to the cause.

What have we learned from this discourse? Well, while Casey Stengel may not have been the greatest of Yankees managers, he certainly is the pivotal figure among the greats. Ralph Houk made a conscious effort to avoid being like Stengel. Billy Martin was both like and unlike Stengel. Joe Torre, except for his personality, almost seems like the second coming of Stengel. Joe McCarthy won many championships. Stengel also won many championships, in addition to many friends who greatly admired him. If you combine management skills and style, it is easy to understand why Stengel is so beloved and usually mentioned ahead of McCarthy in the hierarchy of great Yankees managers.

On the wall in my office, I have a picture that a policeman made — it's me with Miller Huggins, Joe McCarthy, Casey Stengel and Billy Martin. That's pretty good company for me. What would be even more flattering is if the "Major," Ralph Houk, also was in the picture. Every time I achieve a milestone now, it seems to put me in the same company as Houk.

I came to New York in 1996 to manage the Yankees, certainly feeling like, You're walking on sacred ground. You don't belong here. Because of the deep tradition of the Yankees, the idea of being somewhere special has passed from generation to generation. With what has happened in the years since I arrived, at least now I feel comfortable walking in here and feeling like I belong.

How I match up against other managers or how my teams match up against other teams is for historians to decide. Huggins and McCarthy were in a class of their own, obviously, and Martin was excellent at getting a lot of mileage out of players.

Stengel was unique. His clubs were dynamite, always based on power. Well, power and pitching. Casey's teams did a lot of things that scared people. They had guys like Enos Slaughter, who really was more of a line-drive hitter than a traditional power hitter. John Blanchard, who was primarily a pinch-hitter because they didn't have the DH rule back then, hit 21 home runs in 1961. He did that as a second-string catcher. The Yankees brought in a person that had led the league in homers, Johnny Mize. Then you had the Mantles and Yogis.

I think a Stengel team would fare just fine in today's game. Even though Casey's teams hit a huge number of home runs, they didn't strike out any-where near what we tolerate now. I watched those teams from the time I was a 10-year-old kid into my teenage years. To me, Stengel's Yankees were like a machine: They were efficient, and they rarely lost.

Even more so than offensively, Casey's teams would do well today because his pitchers would have thrived in any era. Starting pitchers in those days typically would work 250 innings and more, and they would throw batting practice on the day before their scheduled start. That was a starter's in-between workout: tossing BP. You can't even comprehend such a thing now, considering how we protect pitchers. If you matched Casey's rotation against today's hitters, I suspect the pitchers would do very well.

How would our Yankees have done back then? I think our guys would have been just as good as they are now. My Yankees clubs have been as solid as there ever have been. It's not like we were a fluke one season, or that our payroll put us far above the competition. We've done things right for an extended period, and as a result we have achieved success. In that sense, neither baseball nor the Yankees has changed.

Just having marquee players, back then or now, is not enough. You need to have a team that can play as a unit. You build a seven-run lead now, and you can kiss it good-bye in many cases. You still need good pitching, as Casey's teams had and as ours have had, or you have no chance. The good teams then and now have the best pitching. Good pitchers have consistently intimidated the opposition across all eras, more so than an imposing offense.

— *Joe Torre*

61

*the*
# GREATEST ACHIEVEMENTS

## LOU GEHRIG'S HEROISM AND WHY HE STILL MATTERS
*— Essay by Ray Robinson*

## WHEN THE IRON HORSE BUCKLED
*— Essay by Keith Olbermann*

## THE TOP 25 MOMENTS, MARKS AND EVENTS
Selected by the New York–New Jersey Chapter of the Baseball Writers Association of America
*— Essay by Ken Leiker and Ken Shouler*

*For a team that has won so often for so long, the most memorable events,*

*moments and performances become decidedly relative. Each new season*

*produces its share of moments, though always against the backdrop of what*

*has come before. The New York–New Jersey Chapter of the Baseball Writers*

*Association of America voted on 25 of the most compelling Yankee's memories.*

*Author and historian Ray Robinson's essay centers on a man that matters*

*as much today as he did more than 60 years ago. Keith Olbermann recounts*

*a prescient conversation with the man who replaced Gehrig at first base for*

*the Yankees, and how he saw the signs of a debilitating disease in Gehrig years*

*before Gehrig was forced to give up the game. Ken Leiker and Ken Shouler*

*revisit moments, events, and performances that bring to life the history*

*of sport's greatest franchise.*

NY

HITS
2,721

GAMES
2,164

HOME RUNS
493

GAMES PLAYED
**2,164**
CONSECUTIVELY

RBI
1,995

RUNS
1,888

AVERAGE
.340

1923–1939

*Iron Horse*

# LOU GEHRIG'S
## HEROISM AND WHY
## HE STILL MATTERS

*Essay by Ray Robinson*

The seemingly indestructible Lou Gehrig,
the Percheron-esque first baseman of the
New York Yankees from 1925 to 1939, spent his
Major League Baseball career in the shadow
of those other Yankees icons, Babe Ruth and Joe
DiMaggio. The Babe, certainly the most
implausible sports figure of all time, became
the savior of baseball after eight Chicago White
Sox players fixed the outcome of the 1919
World Series between the White Sox and the
Cincinnati Reds. Ruth's towering and frequent
home runs and outsized persona quickly made
people forget the game's loss of innocence.

ehrig and Ruth were close friends in their first years together with the Yankees, but it was inevitable that their striking personality differences would polarize them. Gehrig never could fully appreciate the Babe's uninhibited carousing and bombast, even as the public preferred the Rabelaisian Ruth to the introverted Gehrig.

"The Babe took a host of Walter Mittys with him as he rounded the bases," historian Bruce Catton wrote. Gehrig, though one of the most productive ballplayers of all time, did not arouse such fantasies in fans. Even on the day in 1932 when he became the first player of the 20th Century to hit four home runs in a game, Gehrig took a backseat. John McGraw picked that same day to resign his 30-year position as manager of the New York Giants. McGraw was in all the headlines of New York City's newspapers, while reports of Gehrig's four home runs in a Philadelphia ballpark received little coverage.

DiMaggio came along in the 1930s. The enigmatic and elegant young center fielder quickly stole the attention away from Gehrig, even though Gehrig was the Yankees captain. DiMaggio was the type of smooth performer who attracted everyone's eye. All Gehrig could offer was his daily commitment to show up on time and play as well as he possibly could. Gehrig was the rock in the Yankees lineup, but DiMaggio with his incredible batting eye, flawless fielding ability, and a natural appeal to a growing number of Italian-American fans, quickly won more headlines and more money.

Despite being relegated to the role of second fiddle for most of his career, Gehrig would seem today to possess a legacy every bit as enduring as that of Ruth or DiMaggio. This is sadly due in no small part to the sudden, tragic cutoff to Gehrig's consecutive games streak at 2,130, and the manner

in which he confronted certain death at a young age.

It was between games of a doubleheader at Yankee Stadium on July 4, 1939, that the diffident Gehrig, dying of amyotrophic lateral sclerosis, a disease that would later bear his name, delivered a farewell speech that became baseball's most eloquent and remembered address. The speech was rendered with such dignity and honesty (and without notes, although the previous night Gehrig's wife, Eleanor, had helped him construct an outline), that it is included in many compendiums of memorable speeches.

Commenting on the speech and its impact, author Wilfrid Sheed wrote: "All present in Yankee Stadium that day had been given a license to love a fellow human being to the limit, without qualifications, and to root for that person as they had never rooted for themselves. If the Stadium had emptied out suddenly, and he had been left standing there alone, Gehrig would have felt no less lucky, because the appearance merely confirmed what he already knew — that he was having a very good day . . . a day like that was worth a thousand of the old ones."

I was present on that melancholic occasion in 1939, a 19-year-old Gehrig fan among the 60,000 or so who had turned out at Yankee Stadium. Some years earlier, as a kid in a Manhattan public school, I had written a letter to Gehrig asking if I might interview him for my

school newspaper. He replied almost at once, employing a penmanship surprisingly delicate for a person of such strength. "I'll be happy to talk to you," wrote Gehrig. "Just use this letter to come to our clubhouse."

Unfortunately, when I journeyed with a friend to Yankee Stadium the following day, we were denied entrance to the sacred enclave of the Yankees clubhouse. Certainly, if we had not been so young and naive — was Gehrig equally naive in

this instance? — we would have anticipated that we'd be turned away, even with the precious letter from Gehrig in hand. We waited outside the Stadium all afternoon, listening eagerly for crowd noises that might have hinted how the Yankees of those glory days were doing. When we heard a swelling roar, we were convinced that Gehrig must have hit a home run. As the sun went down, the game was over, and some time later Gehrig strode out into the street, a man in the prime of his life.

He was, as I still remember, deeply tanned, and his thick brown hair was damp from his postgame shower. I waved his letter, and Gehrig stopped. Taking a quick glance at the paper, he realized he had written it.

"Did you enjoy the game?" Gehrig asked.

We responded with some embarrassment that we had not been admitted into the ballpark. Gehrig appeared genuinely sorry, but he added that he was in a hurry. "I'd be happy to give you the interview some other time," he said. He reached into his pocket and pulled out a pair of crumpled tickets. "These will be good for another day," he said, handing them to us. With that, he waved at us and was gone.

Here I am, some 70 years later, and I still recall the incident with clarity. It inspired me to write a biography of Gehrig, and I can only hope that it was a fair-minded assessment of the man.

From among the greatest Yankees, Gehrig was the native New Yorker, until Whitey Ford came along in 1950. Gehrig was born on June 19, 1903, in Manhattan's Yorkville section, the only child of Christina and Heinrich Gehrig to survive infancy. Money was hard to come by in the Gehrig household, but Christina, who took on odd jobs to provide for the family, adamantly rejected the notion that the Gehrigs were poor. Heinrich had mechanical skills and earned decent wages when he worked, but often he was more devoted to the pursuit of beer, causing him to miss many workdays. One can't escape the irony here, for Gehrig ultimately won a large measure of his fame as baseball's most durable man, a fellow who never failed to show up for work. Gehrig was devoted to his mother and relied greatly on her well into his 20s, until he met Eleanor Twitchell of Chicago and married her in 1933.

Gehrig excelled at football and baseball as a youth, displaying enough promise in both sports to arouse the interest of Columbia University. Gehrig's parents were beside themselves with joy. They long had dreamed of their son becoming "a college man," envisioning that he would study to be an engineer or an architect, but Columbia wanted him only for its football team.

Indeed, when Gehrig enrolled at Columbia, he played football, both on the line and in the backfield. But it was on the baseball diamond that Gehrig truly distinguished himself. After two years he decided to leave school and join the upstart ballclub in town, the Yankees, who were challenging John McGraw's Giants for New York sports supremacy.

The Yankees, in 1921, paid a bit more than $2,000 to Gehrig's parents for the privilege of having their son join Babe Ruth and other Boston Red Sox luminaries who had been lured to the Yankees. Thus, Gehrig took his place as one of Columbia's three most celebrated dropouts, the other two being American Revolutionary hero

*"The Babe is one fellow and I'm another, and I could never be exactly like him. I don't try, I just go on as I am in my own right."*
**— LOU GEHRIG**

Alexander Hamilton and tough-guy actor James Cagney.

Gehrig's consecutive games streak began on June 1, 1925, and didn't end until May 2, 1939. He played through many painful injuries. It is said that at one time or another each of his fingers was broken. He once suffered a concussion from a beanball in an exhibition game but made the Yankees lineup the following day.

Gehrig hit 493 home runs and compiled a batting average of .340. He was one of the most prolific run-producers in history, with seasons of 175, 174, and 184 RBI.

Yet all the while, the outsized Ruth out-roared, out-ate, out-publicized and out-drank entire platoons of ballplayers, including the reserved Gehrig.

Gehrig didn't share publicly his feelings about Ruth. Gehrig was not one to engage in shouting matches, and his ego always took second place to his profound sense of himself as a responsible public figure. This self-imposed role may have at times cost him dearly in his relationships with teammates, opponents, and the ubiquitous media. Certainly his relationship with the Babe, whom Gehrig worshiped for a time, was severely damaged by Ruth's outspoken disparagement of the consecutive games streak. "The streak is a lot of baloney," Ruth had publicly announced, a cut that no doubt hurt Gehrig deeply.

The consecutive games streak ended rather abruptly. Gehrig had a subpar season in 1938, batting less than .300 for the first time since 1925. He went to 1939 spring training determined to regain his form, but his body seemed to be in revolt. His wife referred to it as "a creeping mystery."

"I'm just not feeling right," Gehrig would say. One afternoon in spring training, he climbed atop a bench to gaze out of a clubhouse window, lost his balance, and fell awkwardly backward, landing painfully on his back. Pitcher Wes Ferrell asked Gehrig if he was hurt, and Gehrig tried to brush off the incident as an accident. Ferrell, however, sensed an uncertainty in Gehrig's tone. The following day the two men played golf together, and Ferrell noticed that Gehrig was wearing tennis sneakers instead of golf cleats. "Lou was shuffling his feet as he played," Ferrell said. "It was not pleasant to watch."

A week into the 1939 season, Gehrig was not only failing as a ballplayer, but was also having trouble performing tasks such as tying his shoes and shuffling a deck of playing cards. In Detroit, for a series with the Tigers, Gehrig approached Yankees manager Joe McCarthy, who respected Gehrig more than any other player who ever worked under him, and told him what McCarthy fully anticipated Gehrig was about to say.

"I'm going to bench myself," Gehrig said hoarsely. After a moment's silence, McCarthy asked, "Why, Lou?"

"For the good of the team, Joe. Nobody has to tell me how bad I've been and how much of a drawback I've been to the club. I've been thinking ever since the season opened, when I couldn't start the way I hoped I would, that maybe the time has come for me to quit."

McCarthy understood, yet it was difficult for him, too, to let go. "Take some time off, maybe you'll feel better in a week or so," he said. "Any time you want to get back in there, it's still your job."

The following day, May 2, Ellsworth "Babe" Dahlgren, a slick-fielding first baseman, was assigned the unenviable task of succeeding Gehrig, baseball's Rock of Gibraltar. Gehrig never would play again.

At this critical moment in his life, Gehrig wrote Eleanor a letter, revealing the depth of his feeling for his wife and his own sensitivity to the cloud over his future. This is part of what Gehrig wrote to Eleanor:

*"My Sweetheart — and please grant that we may ever be such, for what the hell else matters — that thing yesterday I believe and hope was the turning point of my life for the future as far as taking life too seriously is concerned. It was inevitable, although I dreaded the day, and my thoughts were with you constantly — and how the thing would affect you and I that was the big question and the most important thought underlying everything. I broke before the game because I thought so much of you. Not because I didn't know you are the bravest kind of partner but because my inferiority grabbed me and made me wonder and ponder if I could possibly prove myself worthy of you. As for me, the road may come to a dead end here, but why should it? Seems like our back is to the wall now, but there usually comes a way out. Where and what, I know not, but who can tell that it might not lead to better things. Time will tell."*

*LG*

# WHEN THE IRON HORSE BUCKLED

ESSAY BY **KEITH OLBERMANN**

On a wet afternoon at Fenway Park in 1935, Lou Gehrig rapped a single to right field and rounded the first base bag. His spikes slid across the slick base and jammed into the muddy infield. Gehrig fell, and he did not rise immediately.

The rookie first baseman of the Red Sox was startled that Gehrig did not seem able to get up. The Yankees captain lay in the mud, one foot stretched back to the base. *That's funny*, the rookie thought to himself. *He's the Iron Horse, he never misses a game, he doesn't look hurt. Something's wrong with him.*

Finally, the rookie spoke up: "Lou? Can I help you?"

The response was muffled. "Just let me take care of it," Gehrig said. He flattened his palms and pushed himself up with his fingers and knees. Once on his feet again, Gehrig wiped his hands on his pants legs and breathed deeply. He smiled wanly at the rookie. "Thanks, kid. What's your name again?"

The rookie swallowed hard. "Lou, I'm Dahlgren," he said. "Babe Dahlgren."

Less than four years later, on May 2, 1939, Dahlgren would succeed Gehrig as first baseman for the Yankees, after Gehrig decided he no longer could help the team and ended his playing streak at 2,130 games. A few weeks later, Gehrig was diagnosed with amyotrophic lateral sclerosis, an incurable disease that breaks down the nerves and tissues of the body.

Half a century later, on May 2, 1989, Dahlgren related the Fenway Park incident to me in an interview on a Los Angeles television station. His memory of Gehrig's struggle to rise from the mud brought up the question: When did the disease that killed Gehrig first begin to eat away at his body?

"I've always thought in my heart that maybe this thing was acting on him as early as '35," Dahlgren told me.

"He was probably sick in 1935. I think I knew something was really wrong when the Yankees bought me (in 1937). Me? What did they need me for? I was really upset when they got me. I thought I'd never play. Then in my mind I saw Lou in the mud like that, not able to get up. And I knew something was terribly wrong. And I think we all knew."

If Gehrig truly was in the early stages of his disease in 1935, what he did the rest of his career was nothing short of incredible. He continued to play every day, in 626 consecutive games. He hit 145 home runs, drove in 545 runs, batted .330. He was the Most Valuable Player in 1936. All perhaps while he was dying.

On the day he replaced Gehrig, Dahlgren dropped down next to the Iron Horse in the dugout in the seventh inning of what would be a 22-2 Yankees victory. Dahlgren urged Gehrig to reconsider and keep the streak alive. "I told him he wouldn't be hurting the team, that this'd at least give him another day to get better. He just smiled and told me the team was doing fine, and shook my hand."

Dahlgren repeated his request to Gehrig in the eighth inning, and again his idol turned him down. Before heading out to the field for the bottom of the ninth, Dahlgren made one final plea. "I asked him to do it for me, that I didn't want to be the one to break his streak. I put it on those terms."

Gehrig's opaque eyes gazed past Dahlgren. "I appreciate it, Babe," he said. "But I'm done."

Gehrig went to the Mayo Clinic in Minnesota to find out what was wrong with him. The diagnosis, couched in the sterile, bloodless language of medical speak, was dreadful. He was suffering from amyotrophic lateral sclerosis, an incurable and relatively unknown disease. It was never clear if Gehrig knew he had been handed a death sentence. Eleanor knew; the Mayo doctors had told her. It is possible that she chose to withhold the news from her husband. Yet, it is not unreasonable to assume that as Gehrig's body continued to fail, even though his brain remained sharp and alert, he was aware of the hopelessness of his condition.

Gehrig remained with the Yankees for the rest of the 1939 season, traveling with the team

*"I had him for over eight years and he never gave me a moment's trouble. I guess you might say he was kind of my favorite."*

**— JOE McCARTHY,**
**Yankees manager (right)**

and holding his title of team captain, even though his playing days were over. While the Yankees were beating the Cincinnati Reds in the World Series, Gehrig was becoming acquainted with New York mayor Fiorello LaGuardia, who was so impressed with Gehrig's intelligence and tenacity that he offered him a post on the New York City parole commission. The mayor reasoned that the famous Gehrig might be an inspiration to the city's wayward youngsters in need of rehabilitation.

After some reluctance because he didn't feel he was qualified for the position, Gehrig accepted and delved into books on criminology, psychology and sociology with the same dedication and enthusiasm that he had played baseball. The pay for his new job was $5,700 a year; not a meager

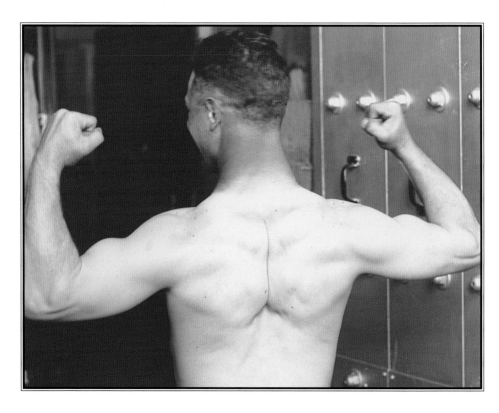

stipend at the time, but only a few dollars more than Gehrig's share of the 1939 World Series proceeds.

Gehrig earned the reputation of a thoughtful man in his new role. He seemed inclined to give many a second chance and was never excessively punitive. "We must play fair with these fellows," he said. "But we must also consider the rights of the taxpayers and our duties toward them. We don't want anyone in jail who can make good."

One person who failed to gain Gehrig's compassion was 19-year-old Rocco Barbella; a swaggering hoodlum who had been incarcerated on a statutory rape charge. Gehrig studied Barbella's case conscientiously, and it was clear to him that Barbella had caused his mother considerable grief.

*"Lou was the kind of boy that if you had a son, he's the kind of person you would like your son to be."*

— **SAM JONES, teammate**

This weighed heavily on Gehrig, whose loyalty and lifetime devotion to his mother was legendary. Gehrig's decision was swift: Barbella was to be returned to reform school. As he was taken away, the enraged Barbella shouted at Gehrig that he was a "bastard." Years later, Barbella became Rocky Graziano, a hugely successful and popular middleweight boxing champion, and he credited Gehrig for helping "to straighten me out."

By the spring of 1941 Gehrig's relentless disease had destroyed his body to the point where he could no longer perform his parole board assignment satisfactorily. Eleanor had been his chauffeur, driving him every morning to his office in lower Manhattan. His legs, once sturdy and fleet enough that he stole home 15 times in the major

*"I'm not a headline guy. I know that as long as I was following Ruth to the plate, I could have stood on my head and no one would have known the difference."*

— **LOU GEHRIG**

HR 49
RBI 165
AVG. .363
TRIPLE CROWN
1936
AMERICAN LEAGUE

leagues, could no longer bear his weight, and his trembling fingers could not properly sign documents. Yet his mind remained active and attentive. Neurologists who have treated this incurable disease say that for the victim it is like attending his own funeral.

On June 2, 1941, 17 days before his 38th birthday, Gehrig died in his sleep at home. It had been a little more than two years since his condition had been diagnosed at the Mayo Clinic. President Franklin D. Roosevelt, himself a survivor of polio and a man with a fondness for baseball, sent flowers. LaGuardia ordered that all New York City flags be flown at half-mast. At Gehrig's funeral, his long-time on-the-road roommate with the Yankees, catcher Bill Dickey, succinctly summed up the feelings of those who had known Gehrig. "Lou didn't need tributes from anyone," Dickey said. "His life and the way he lived were tribute enough; he just went out and did his job every day."

*Lou Gehrig with his mother, Christina.*

Save perhaps for Willie Keeler and late-1800s pitcher Mickey Welch, Lou Gehrig was the first New Yorker to star for a New York baseball team since the game went professional after the Civil War.

Babe Ruth was from Baltimore. Christy Mathewson, the idol of the Giants, was from Pennsylvania, as was John Ward, the Giants' 1880s superstar. Keeler, born and raised in Brooklyn, gained most of his fame playing for the Baltimore Orioles, although he also had good seasons with the Dodgers and the Yankees. Welch, from Brooklyn, won 238 games for the Giants. John McGraw of upstate Truxton, the Giants manager for 30 years, was all but done as a player when he left the Orioles.

As a New York homegrown hero, Gehrig has never been truly replaced. Phil Rizzuto and Whitey Ford are New Yorkers, and both are in the Hall of Fame, but neither would claim to be in a league with Gehrig.

Gehrig was the Yankees captain for many years, and for many New Yorkers that title went into the grave with the Iron Horse in 1941. It wasn't until the 1970s that the Yankees again named a captain, a catcher from Ohio named Thurman Munson.

# THE TOP 25
## MOMENTS, MARKS AND EVENTS

*Essays by Ken Leiker and Ken Shouler*

Major League Baseball's integrity was seriously compromised in 1919, when some members of the Chicago White Sox conspired with gamblers and threw the World Series. The plot was unraveled in a courtroom drama the following year, and disbelieving fans expressed betrayal and outrage. Some swore off the game forever; others demanded to know why they should ever again take baseball seriously. As the game's leadership speculated on how badly baseball had been damaged and whether it could thrive again, little did they know that the seeds of recovery were being sown.

> "No other club could afford to give the amount the Yankees have paid for him,
> **AND I DO NOT MIND SAYING I THINK THEY ARE TAKING A GAMBLE.**
> The Boston club can now go into the market and buy other players and have a stronger
> and better team than if Ruth had remained with us."
>
> — HARRY FRAZEE, Red Sox owner, when Ruth's sale to the Yankees was announced

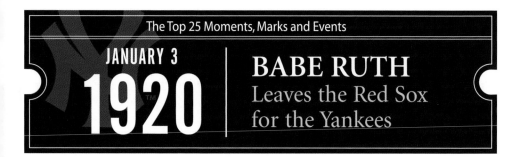

The Top 25 Moments, Marks and Events

**JANUARY 3**

# 1920

# BABE RUTH
## Leaves the Red Sox for the Yankees

On the day after Christmas, in 1919, Harry Frazee unwittingly saved baseball. Frazee's intentions were not so pure when he arranged a clandestine meeting that day with the principals of the New York Yankees, whose office was within shouting distance of his own in New York's theater district. Frazee, owner of the Boston Red Sox — baseball's most successful team over the first two decades of the 20th Century; winners of five of the first 15 World Series — had two problems: mounting debt and a charismatic, pigeon-toed slugger who was demanding that his salary be doubled.

Within hours Frazee had signed over Babe Ruth's contract to the Yankees in exchange for $125,000 in cash and a $300,000 loan with Fenway Park as collateral. (The deal wasn't announced until January 3, 1920.) The cash was twice what any player had fetched previously in a sale, but it would prove to be baseball's greatest bargain. Ruth was the best left-handed pitcher of the era and so accomplished a hitter that the Red Sox had taken to using him in the outfield when he wasn't pitching. Upon arriving in New York, he succeeded in getting his salary doubled to $20,000, then took on a larger-than-life status, booming home runs at a stunning clip and living equally large off the field. Fans forgave baseball its transgressions and returned to

ballparks in droves to see the Babe, who became one of the defining symbols of the Roaring '20s. In 1920 the Yankees became the first team to surpass 1 million in home attendance, and within a few years the Yankees were the most powerful and famous team in baseball, representing the most powerful and influential city in the world.

Ruth's role in luring fans back to baseball cannot be overestimated. Performing at a level above his peers, which has never been matched by any athlete in any sport — and likely never will be — he was an irresistible attraction. Consider the following: Ruth hit 54 home runs in his first season with the Yankees, more than the total of any team except his own and the Philadelphia Phillies; when he hit his 700th homer, no one else had hit even 300; and when he died in 1948, he held 56 major league records.

As for Frazee, he remains a reviled figure in New England lore for his role in shifting baseball's balance of baseball power from Boston to New York. The Red Sox trail the Yankees 26-0 in World Series titles since Ruth moved south. The Babe's legend was growing to mythic proportions in New York, when one day Frazee hailed a Boston taxi for a ride to Fenway Park. Upon learning the identity of his passenger, the cabbie took a swing for all of New England. He dropped Frazee with one punch.

America never has been riveted to baseball quite like it was for two months in the summer of 1941. It was an unsettling time in the world, the uneasy calm before the storm. Hitler and the Nazis ruled Germany and were plotting to take the rest of Europe. The Japanese were the silent enemy across the Pacific. President Roosevelt challenged Congress to prepare for national defense. The American public needed respite from the grim news of the real world and found it in a sporting drama that became more gripping with each passing day. "Did he get a hit?" became the most popular refrain in the country.

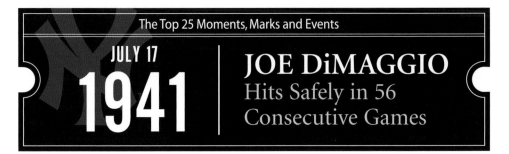

**The Top 25 Moments, Marks and Events**

**JULY 17**
# 1941

# JOE DiMAGGIO
## Hits Safely in 56 Consecutive Games

Joe DiMaggio, the gifted and graceful center fielder of the mighty New York Yankees, was getting a hit every day. Starting on May 15, 1941, and winding through June and into July, DiMaggio hit safely in 56 consecutive games, a streak that many regard as the most remarkable achievement in sports history. More than 60 years have passed since DiMaggio's feat, and no one has come closer than 44 games. That's still 20 percent short, two weeks' worth of games.

DiMaggio's streak was the signature achievement of his sterling career, yet it served to measure him more as an American icon than a ballplayer, broadening an audience that was mesmerized by his excellence, elegance, and charisma. Except for Babe Ruth, no ballplayer has ever captivated and fascinated the American public like DiMaggio did. He was poised, confident, proud, humble, detached, seemingly above human frailties. He rarely showed emotion on the field, reacting to success and failure in the same stoic manner. Baseball contemporaries spoke of him in reverent tones. DiMaggio never disappointed his adoring public, yet he was a private man who left much unsaid,

which only added to the mystique about him.

DiMaggio was performing like a common ballplayer before he launched his 1941 hitting streak on May 15, batting only .306 after batting-championship seasons of .381 in 1939 and .352 in 1940. He had few close calls in the streak, needing a hit in his final at-bat only a few times. When pitchers became loath to throw DiMaggio strikes, Yankees manager Joe McCarthy allowed him to swing away on 3-and-0 counts. DiMaggio had a .408 batting average (91 for 223), 15 homers and 55 RBI during the streak, and after it ended he had a hit in each of the next 16 games, which meant that he had hit safely in 72 of 73 games.

The 56-game streak ended on July 17 in Cleveland, in front of a crowd of more than 67,000. Indians third baseman Ken Keltner twice robbed DiMaggio of hits. In his final at-bat, DiMaggio sent a hard grounder to the left side that kicked up late, but shortstop Lou Boudreau was able to snatch the ball near his shoulder and flip to second baseman Ray Mack in time to start a double play. Befitting his image, DiMaggio showed no emotion, taking the disappointment "like a man," as the saying went.

## LONGEST HITTING STREAKS

| PLAYER | YEAR | TEAM | STREAK |
|---|---|---|---|
| Joe DiMaggio | 1941 | New York (AL) | 56 |
| Willie Keeler | 1897 | Baltimore (NL) | 44 |
| Pete Rose | 1978 | Cincinnati | 44 |
| Bill Dahlen | 1894 | Chicago (NL) | 42 |
| George Sisler | 1922 | St. Louis (AL) | 41 |
| Ty Cobb | 1911 | Detroit | 40 |
| Paul Molitor | 1987 | Milwaukee (AL) | 39 |
| Tommy Holmes | 1945 | Boston (NL) | 37 |
| Billy Hamilton | 1894 | Philadelphia (NL) | 36 |
| Fred Clarke | 1895 | Louisville (NL) | 35 |
| Ty Cobb | 1917 | Detroit | 35 |
| Luis Castillo | 2002 | Florida | 35 |
| George Sisler | 1925 | St. Louis (AL) | 34 |
| George McQuinn | 1938 | St. Louis (AL) | 34 |
| Dom DiMaggio | 1949 | Boston (AL) | 34 |
| Benito Santiago | 1987 | San Diego | 34 |
| George Davis | 1893 | New York (NL) | 33 |
| Hal Chase | 1907 | New York (AL) | 33 |
| Rogers Hornsby | 1922 | St. Louis (NL) | 33 |
| Heinie Manush | 1933 | Washington | 33 |
| Ed Delahanty | 1899 | Philadelphia (NL) | 31 |
| Nap Lajoie | 1906 | Cleveland | 31 |
| Sam Rice | 1924 | Washington | 31 |
| Willie Davis | 1969 | Los Angeles | 31 |
| Rico Carty | 1970 | Atlanta | 31 |
| Ken Landreaux | 1980 | Minnesota | 31 |
| Vladimir Guerrero | 1999 | Montreal | 31 |
| Cal McVey | 1876 | Chicago (NL) | 30 |
| Elmer Smith | 1898 | Cincinnati | 30 |
| Tris Speaker | 1912 | Boston (AL) | 30 |
| Goose Goslin | 1934 | Detroit | 30 |
| Stan Musial | 1950 | St. Louis (NL) | 30 |
| Ron LeFlore | 1976 | Detroit | 30 |
| George Brett | 1980 | Kansas City | 30 |
| Jerome Walton | 1989 | Chicago (NL) | 30 |
| Sandy Alomar Jr. | 1997 | Cleveland | 30 |
| Nomar Garciaparra | 1997 | Boston | 30 |
| Eric Davis | 1998 | Baltimore | 30 |
| Luis Gonzalez | 1999 | Arizona | 30 |
| Albert Pujols | 2003 | St. Louis | 30 |

When it came to hitting a baseball in the 1920s, every batter but one felt the fierce tug of gravity. Babe Ruth was on a different level, above the exosphere, his head poking through the ether, competing at a level of his own making. A new headline language of wallops and swats, clouts and blasts, booms and bams was invented to describe his feats.

## SEPTEMBER 30
# 1927

# BABE RUTH
Takes the Home Run
Record to 60

Ruth changed the game by taking quantum leap upon quantum leap over his peers. His 29 home runs in 1919 set an all-time record. His 54 the following year shattered the previous record that had defined baseball; the next man in line hit 19. Just one of 15 teams beside his Yankees hit as many as Ruth hit alone. The runner-up hit 24 in 1921 and couldn't see Ruth in the distance; Babe hit 59.

Few measured Ruth against others. Ruth was the Sultan of Swat and would forever be judged, trapped even, by the lofty standards he set in his mid-20s. Whatever the reasons — peerless fame, wealth (his income from baseball, motion pictures, vaudeville, barnstorming, syndicated ghost-written columns and endorsements was more than $250,000 in 1926) or insatiable indulgence — Ruth didn't approach his record of 59 for five years. How likely was it that Ruth, his girth swelling, would set a new standard in 1927?

Ruth was motivated by a painful loss to the St. Louis Cardinals in the 1926 Series. He tried to steal second base and was thrown out — the final out of the Yankees' one-run loss in Game 7. "The only dumb play I ever saw you make," Yankees general manager Ed Barrow told Ruth.

Ruth had 43 homers when the 1927 calendar flipped to September, and he hit nine in the following two weeks. The Yankees clinched the pennant on September 13 and would win 110 games. One drama remained: Could Ruth hit eight home runs in the remaining 14 games? He tied his record of 59 by hitting two on the third-to-last day of the season.

The following game, on September 30, Ruth connected with a low, inside fastball from Tom Zachary of the Washington Senators and drove it just inside the right-field foul pole and halfway up the bleachers in Yankee Stadium. Hats and confetti rained onto the field. As Ruth went to right field for the next inning, he received a handkerchief salute from the bleacher denizens. Ruth playfully returned a series of military salutes.

In the clubhouse after the game, Ruth bellowed, "60 homers! — let's see some sonofabitch match that." Nobody did for 34 years.

There were 152,666 major league games played in the 20th Century, which means that 305,332 pitchers had an opportunity to achieve a perfect game — retiring all batters without any of them reaching base. Only 15 did.

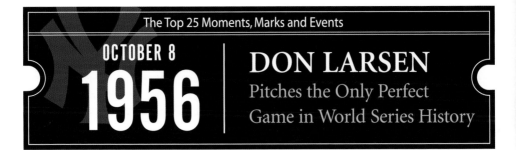

## OCTOBER 8
# 1956

# DON LARSEN
## Pitches the Only Perfect
## Game in World Series History

On average, it happened once every seven years, once every 10,900 games. The list of 15 includes five Hall of Fame pitchers — but it does not include the likes of Christy Mathewson, Lefty Grove, Grover Cleveland Alexander, Warren Spahn, Walter Johnson, Roger Clemens, Steve Carlton, Whitey Ford, Nolan Ryan, Bob Gibson or Tom Seaver. Those immortals on their greatest day were not as good as Don Larsen was on his greatest day. Even among the perfect-game pitchers, Larsen stands alone, for he was the only one to achieve the feat on baseball's biggest stage, the World Series. No one else, in fact, has ever pitched a no-hitter in the World Series or in the postseason series that now precede it.

Larsen pitched for 14 seasons in the major leagues and ended his career with a modest 81-91 record. One year he went 3-21. For every nine innings he pitched, he gave up an average of eight hits and four walks. Larsen clearly had talent, but he also had a reputation for losing focus and purpose on the mound. Teammates called him "Gooneybird." He was a voracious reader of comic books and had an affinity for the nightlife. After Larsen wrecked his car during the wee hours of the morning one spring, Yankees manager Casey Stengel deadpanned, "He must've been going to the post office to mail a letter."

If a New York Yankees pitcher was destined to achieve perfection in 1956, it surely would have been 19-game winner Whitey Ford, 18-game winner Johnny Kucks or 16-game winner Tom Sturdivant. Larsen went 11-5 — it would prove to be the best season of his career — but he didn't make it through the second inning against the Brooklyn Dodgers in the second game of the World Series. Stengel sent out Larsen again for the fifth game on the afternoon of October 8.

No one, least of all Larsen, knows what came over him that day. He worked from a stretch position because he had lost confidence in his ability to pitch from a traditional windup. Inning by inning, batter by batter, he pitched with the skill, guile, and poise he had never known. Larsen sat down a lineup that included Jackie Robinson, Pee Wee Reese, Duke Snider and Roy Campanella, all Hall of Fame–bound players. He went to a ball-three count only once, and the Yankees made only three plays behind him that were considered above the norm.

For two hours and six minutes, the 27-year-old Larsen practiced the craft of pitching better than almost anyone ever had. When it was over, the Yankees had a 2-0 victory and the tall, broad-shouldered Larsen had Yogi Berra in his arms, a celebratory embrace that is one of the most lasting sports images of the era. The next year, the perfect pitcher became Don Larsen again, a condition he could live with because he had proved there is a cure: Anything was possible.

Here is the Brooklyn Dodgers lineup that Don Larsen faced on October 8, 1956, and their statistics for the regular season.

Reese, Snider, Robinson and Campanella are in the Hall of Fame.

| PLAYER | POS | G | HR | RBI | SB | BA | PLAYER | POS | G | HR | RBI | SB | BA |
|---|---|---|---|---|---|---|---|---|---|---|---|---|---|
| Junior Gilliam | 2B | 153 | 6 | 43 | 21 | .300 | Sandy Amoros | LF | 114 | 16 | 58 | 3 | .260 |
| Pee Wee Reese | SS | 147 | 9 | 46 | 13 | .257 | Carl Furillo | RF | 149 | 21 | 83 | 1 | .289 |
| Duke Snider | CF | 151 | 43 | 101 | 3 | .292 | Roy Campanella | C | 124 | 20 | 73 | 1 | .219 |
| Jackie Robinson | 3B | 117 | 10 | 43 | 12 | .275 | Sal Maglie | P | 28 | 0 | 2 | 0 | .129 |
| Gil Hodges | 1B | 153 | 32 | 87 | 3 | .265 | Dale Mitchell | PH | 57 | 0 | 7 | 0 | .204 |

Roger Maris arrived in Keokuk, Iowa, during the summer of 1954, climbing the minor-league ladder. Keokuk manager Jo-Jo White watched the strapping, young left-handed batter hitting the ball to all fields and quickly interrupted. "Look, boy," White bellowed, "you're not a singles hitter. You're big and you've got power. Pull that ball to right field and see what happens."

## BEST TO NEXT

Roger Maris' second-best home run total was 39. The following list shows players who had the greatest difference between their best and second-best home run seasons.

| PLAYER | BEST | SECOND BEST | DIFF. |
|---|---|---|---|
| Brady Anderson | 50 (1996) | 24 (1999) | 26 |
| Luis Gonzalez | 57 (2001) | 31 (2000) | 26 |
| Davey Johnson | 43 (1973) | 18 (1971) | 25 |
| Barry Bonds | 73 (2001) | 49 (2000) | 24 |
| Roger Maris | 61 (1961) | 39 (1960) | 22 |
| Joe Charboneau | 23 (1980) | 4 (1981) | 19 |
| Ken Hunt | 25 (1961) | 6 (1963) | 19 |
| Terry Steinbach | 35 (1996) | 16 (1987) | 19 |
| Willard Marshall | 36 (1947) | 17 (1953) | 19 |
| Buzz Arlett | 18 (1931) | ——— | 18 |
| Bob Cerv | 38 (1958) | 20 (1959) | 18 |
| Jim Baxes | 17 (1959) | ——— | 17 |
| Jay Bell | 38 (1999) | 21 (1997) | 17 |
| Andre Dawson | 49 (1987) | 32 (1983) | 17 |
| Hack Wilson | 56 (1930) | 39 (1929) | 17 |

# OCTOBER 1
# 1961

## ROGER MARIS
### Hits 61 Home Runs

White's sage advice would carry Maris to unprecedented heights in the game — and also bring him unwarranted pain and revilement.

No other ballplayer has ever pulled the ball quite as effectively and efficiently as Maris did during the 1961 season. He had joined the New York Yankees the previous season and proved to be a fine player. Maris played with a burning intensity, was a superb right fielder with an exceptionally strong arm, and rarely made a mistake while running the bases. But his greatest attribute was a quick pull swing with a slight uppercut that was ideal for Yankee Stadium, where the right field bleachers sat little more than 300 feet from home plate. Few of Maris' home runs traveled as far as 400 feet; most dropped into the early rows of seats in the lower deck of the Stadium.

The 1961 season promised to be an offensive awakening, especially in the American League, which had new teams in Los Angeles and Washington, D.C., and with them at least 20 pitchers who otherwise wouldn't be considered major league quality. In addition, the schedule had been extended from 154 to 162 games. No one, though, expected an assault on the most hallowed record in sport: Babe Ruth's 60 home runs in a season. Maris and his more celebrated teammate, Mickey Mantle, took up the chase, and both were still on pace for the record in late August.

Mantle dropped out in September because of a hip injury, leaving Maris to go it alone. The public and press had been chilly to Maris' mounting home run total, all along favoring Mantle, a larger-than-life and charismatic player in the great tradition of Yankees legends. Once Maris became the only threat to Ruth, the environment about him was charged with hostility and even hatred. The relentless pressure caused his hair to fall out in clumps and turned his personality sour. The career .260 hitter found solace only in the batter's box, where he could slip into the one-on-one battle with a pitcher and erase everything else from his consciousness.

The homers kept coming. On October 1, the final day of the season, the battle-weary Maris connected with a 2-and-0 fastball from Tracy Stallard of the Boston Red Sox and dropped it some 340 feet into the right field seats at Yankee Stadium for his 61st homer. The crowd that day was a mere 23,154, a third of the Stadium's capacity. Baseball almost seemed ashamed of Maris' feat. Commissioner Ford Frick had decreed that Maris would have to set the record in 154 games for it to be official, and Yankees management declined to promote Maris' chase — all in deference to the godlike Ruth, who had held the season home run record for 42 years.

Maris was the first to reach 60 homers in 34 years. And it would be 37 years before both Mark McGwire and Sammy Sosa surpassed Maris' record in 1998.

# GEHRIG'S FAREWELL SPEECH

"FOR THE PAST TWO WEEKS YOU HAVE BEEN READING ABOUT A
BAD BREAK. BUT TODAY I CONSIDER MYSELF THE LUCKIEST MAN
ON THE FACE OF THE EARTH.

I have been in ballparks for 17 years and have never received
anything but kindness and encouragement from you fans.

Look at these grand men. Which of you wouldn't consider it the highlight of his
career just to associate with them for even one day? Sure I'm lucky. Who wouldn't
consider it an honor to have known Jacob Ruppert? Also, the builder of baseball's
greatest empire, Ed Barrow? To have spent six years with that wonderful little
fellow, Miller Huggins? Then to have spent the next nine years with the
best manager in baseball today, Joe McCarthy?

Sure I'm lucky. When the New York Giants, a team you would give your right
arm to beat, and vice versa, sends you a gift — that's something. When
everybody down to the groundskeepers and those boys in white coats
remember you with trophies — that's something.

When you have a wonderful mother-in-law who takes sides with you in
squabbles with her own daughter — that's something. When you have a father
and a mother who work all their lives so you can have an education and build your
body — it's a blessing. When you have a wife who has been a tower of strength and
shown more courage than you dreamed existed — that's the finest I know.

I MIGHT HAVE BEEN GIVEN A BAD BREAK,
BUT I'VE GOT AN AWFUL LOT TO LIVE FOR. THANK YOU."

Few have personified the American Dream like Lou Gehrig did. The son of poor German immigrants, he grew up to be the star first baseman of his hometown New York Yankees, perhaps the best first baseman in history. No matter how rich and famous he became, Gehrig never failed to give his best every day.

The Top 25 Moments, Marks and Events

JULY 4

# 1939

# LOU GEHRIG
Delivers His Farewell
Speach at Yankee Stadium

For 14 years he was as regular as the postman, except the postman got Sunday off and Gehrig didn't. Through it all, he maintained a quiet dignity, never boasting or showing a crass side, never envious of the spotlight dominated by Babe Ruth, his more celebrated teammate. Ruth might be the best ballplayer in history, but he was not the captain of the Yankees. Gehrig was; he engendered that level of respect.

Gehrig's legend began when the Yankees used him as a pinch-hitter on June 1, 1925, and a day later he was playing at first base. The next time he missed a game was May 2, 1939. For 2,130 consecutive games, Gehrig's name appeared in the Yankees boxscore. He played through broken bones, back spasms, concussions, and illness. His hands were X-rayed late in his career, and doctors found 17 different fractures that had healed while Gehrig continued to play. In the history of professional sports, only Cal Ripken Jr. has played in more consecutive games than Gehrig had.

Gehrig was a big man for his era, more than 6 feet tall, 200 pounds. Naturally strong, he had broad shoulders, a powerful back and massive thighs. Gehrig looked every bit the he-man in a double-breasted suit and even better in the pinstriped uniform of the Yankees. His body, however, began to betray him in spring training of 1939. Balls that Gehrig hit right on the screws looped over the infield rather than soar out of the ballpark. His motor skills slipped; he had trouble tying his shoelaces and routine plays at first base required extraordinary effort from him. It got worse after the regular season started, and after eight games Gehrig took himself out of the lineup. He never would play again.

The big man went to the Mayo Clinic in June 1939 and came away with a grim diagnosis: amyotrophic lateral sclerosis, an incurable form of paralysis that destroys the central nervous system and has come to be known as "Lou Gehrig's Disease." He was 36, and he had two years to live.

The story could end right here, and Gehrig would be remembered as one of baseball's greatest treasures. Instead, the chapter that virtually every American has come to know was written on July 4, 1939, Lou Gehrig Appreciation Day at Yankee Stadium. The quiet man stood at home plate and in measured, heartfelt words delivered a message from his soul, the most famous address in baseball history. With dignity and grace, he told more than 60,000 spectators in the stadium and many thousands more listening on the radio: "Today I consider myself the luckiest man on the face of the earth."

The New York Yankees were staging a renaissance of their glorious past in the mid-1970s. Aided by the advent of the free-agent players' market and owner George Steinbrenner's largesse, the Yankees had a good enough team in place to win the American League pennant in 1976, for the first time in 12 years. But losing the World Series to the Cincinnati Reds in four games pushed the determined Steinbrenner to dig even deeper. He was the winning bidder for the services of Reggie Jackson, the ranking power hitter of the day, and the game's most flamboyant personality.

"I must admit: When Reggie hit his third home run and I was sure nobody was looking,

## I APPLAUDED IN MY GLOVE."

**— STEVE GARVEY, after Game 6 of the 1977 World Series**

The Top 25 Moments, Marks and Events

**OCTOBER 18**

**1977**

**REGGIE JACKSON**
Slams Three Home Runs in
Game 6 of the World Series

A mid great fanfare and expectation, Jackson strode into a posh New York hotel on November 29, 1976, took a seat in a gilded chair, and signed what then was the most lucrative contract in baseball history: $2.9 million for five years. Never short on self-promotion, he remarked that he probably would have a candy bar named after him.

Jackson's adjustment to a Yankees team rife with seasoned veterans resentful of his celebrity and managed by the fiery Billy Martin proved to be a summer-long ordeal. Jackson certainly didn't endear himself to his new clubhouse when, prior to the season, he told a magazine writer, "I'm the straw that stirs the drink," adding that respected team captain Thurman Munson "thinks he can be the straw that stirs the drink, but he can only stir it bad."

Yet when they took the field, the Yankees managed to put aside their differences and perform as one. Jackson, most of all, relished the refuge he found four or five times a night when he strode to home plate and cocked his menacing bat. He achieved one of his best seasons — 32 home runs, 110 RBI, 20 game-winning hits — and the Yankees again advanced to the World Series, this time against the Los Angeles Dodgers.

After five games, the Yankees held a 3-2 lead and Jackson had two home runs. As the teams pre-

pared for Game 6 at Yankee Stadium on October 18, Jackson was a man possessed during batting practice, blasting pitch after pitch into the seats. "Save some of those for the game," said Willie Randolph. Jackson shot a glare at his teammate and said defiantly, "There are more where those came from." Were there ever. During the next three hours, Jackson put on the greatest show ever by a batter in the World Series. After walking in his first at-bat, he drilled home runs on the first pitch in each of his next three trips to the plate. The third home run was a majestic blast that soared like a rocket toward center field, cleared the fence, and bounced crazily among the black unoccupied seats — more than 450 feet from home plate. As Jackson circled the bases in his signature swaggering trot, the crowd of 56,407 was deafening in its "Reggie! Reggie! Reggie!" salute. Twenty minutes later, the Yankees clinched their first World Championship since 1962.

Jackson's five home runs — and fourth in four official at-bats going back to the eighth inning of Game 5 — is a record for a World Series. As great a player as he was, he rose to a higher level when performing in October on baseball's grandest stage. Jackson's batting average for his six World Series is 95 points better than his season average (.357 to .262), and his slugging average of .755 is a Series record.

The playoff game mirrored the 1978 season. The Boston Red Sox jumped ahead, seemed to be in control, fell behind, rallied, and fell short. New Yorkers witnessed the Yankees in a wholly unfamiliar role: the underdog. As much as the Yankees had achieved in 75 seasons — including winning 21 World Series — they had never made up so much ground chasing someone else.

The Top 25 Moments, Marks and Events

OCTOBER 2

1978

BUCKY DENT
Puts One Over the
Green Monster

The American League pennant race appeared settled three weeks earlier, during a weekend gruesomely stamped the "Boston Massacre" by Red Sox Nation. No need for the exaggerating effects of time to make that story larger. The weekend assumed mythic dimensions the moment it happened. The Yankees entered Fenway Park, a den of fear for opposing pitchers, and cold-cocked the Red Sox four straight by a score of 42-9. After losing two in Yankee Stadium the following weekend, Boston was 2½ games behind with nine to go.

This reversal was incredible. Boston had been 51-19 and held a 14-game lead on July 19. Following the All-Star break, the Sox lost 11 of 14, and half of their lead disappeared. Meanwhile, the Yankees, under the calming influence of manager Bob Lemon, who had replaced the volatile Billy Martin in late July, won 52 of their last 73 games. The Red Sox regrouped in time, won their final eight games, and pulled even.

In the winner-goes-on, loser-goes-home game on October 2, 1978, the Red Sox sent to the mound Mike Torrez, who had won two World Series games for the Yankees the previous year. Torrez took charge, holding a 2-0 lead into the seventh. It would have been 4-0 except that in the sixth inning, Yankees right fielder Lou Piniella, cheating toward the foul line on a hunch that pitcher Ron Guidry was tiring, snatched Fred Lynn's sizzling line drive before it could reach the right field corner.

Two Yankees reached base in the seventh, and then up came Bucky Dent, the ninth batter in the lineup. Torrez's fastball was much too true. Dent connected and the ball took flight toward the Green Monster in left field. "I didn't know it cleared the wall till I got past first," Dent said of his three-run homer that put the Yankees in charge 3-2.

With a runner on third base, Goose Gossage got the final out for the Yankees in the bottom of the ninth, paralyzing Carl Yastrzemski with a hard-boring fastball that Yaz meekly popped into the air. The final score was 5-4 — ending another chapter in the curse of the Red Sox, who had sold the mighty Babe Ruth to the Yankees in 1920 and were still being punished for such foolhardiness 58 years later.

"You know you dream about things like that when you're a kid.
WELL, MY DREAM CAME TRUE."

— **BUCKY DENT**

> Lou Gehrig went about baseball with such unflagging persistence that he undersold his own magnificence. He was the immutable background rhythm that accentuated Babe Ruth's blare of trumpets.

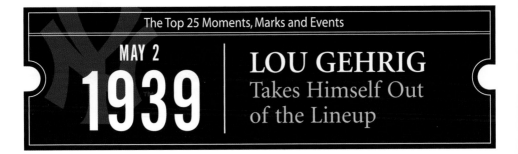

The Top 25 Moments, Marks and Events

MAY 2
1939

# LOU GEHRIG
Takes Himself Out
of the Lineup

Gehrig got his Iron Horse nickname from a superior locomotive of his time. That a 35-year-old man suddenly would lose the singular strength that was the foundation for his streak of consecutive games played was as unlikely as Sir Isaac Newton awakening to find that a propensity for math had deserted him between discovery of the second and third laws of motion. Yet it happened.

Forever second in renown, Gehrig joined a team that had won a World Series and whose celebrity was due to Ruth. Ruth and Gehrig would become the most formidable pair on the same team in baseball history, but there never was any doubt about who held the leading role and who was the supporting actor.

In a fabled 1927 season, the two staged a neck-and-neck race for the home run title. Ruth pulled away in September and prevailed, 60 to 47. In the forlorn words of one writer, "Gehrig was the one who hit all those homers the year Ruth broke the record." In the 1928 World Series, Gehrig swatted a then-record four homers; more often what is recalled is that Ruth hit three in the final game to seal the sweep of the St. Louis Cardinals.

While closing in on Everett Scott's record of 1,307 consecutive games in 1932, Gehrig became the first player in the 20th Century to hit four home runs in a game. John McGraw resigned as the New York Giants manager that same day, so while McGraw made page one, Gehrig made the sports page. Ruth's two homers in the third game of the Series that year, including the famed "called shot," rendered Gehrig's pair in the same game all but forgotten.

For one foreboding month in 1939, Gehrig got all the attention. He had played in every Yankees game from June 1, 1925, to April 30, 1939 — 2,130 consecutive games. But Gehrig was slumping, and when a teammate praised him for a routine play, Gehrig knew the end had come. On May 2, in the Book-Cadillac Hotel in Detroit, he told manager Joe McCarthy of his decision. "I'm going to bench myself," he said. McCarthy asked why. "For the good of the team, Joe," Gehrig said.

Wally Pipp, the player Gehrig replaced 14 years earlier and now a businessman, coincidentally was in the hotel that day. When the announcement that Gehrig wasn't playing in the lineup came over the public address in Detroit's Briggs Stadium, a crowd of 11,000 honored him with a two-minute ovation.

Gehrig's replacement was someone named Babe. Ellsworth "Babe" Dahlgren homered in New York's 22-2 rout of Detroit in that first game without Gehrig, who cried while sitting in the dugout that day. Gehrig never played again. He retired from baseball in June, following the disclosure that he had an illness that would kill him. The Iron Horse had come to a halt, but the Yankees rolled on uninterrupted, winning their fourth consecutive World Series in 1939.

On May 2, in the Book-Cadillac Hotel in Detroit,
Gehrig told manager Joe McCarthy of his decision:

"I'M GOING TO BENCH MYSELF."

Chambliss dug in, connected on the first pitch from Mark Littell, **AND LIFTED A TANTALIZING FLY TO RIGHT FIELD.**

A home run by Chris Chambliss, the Yankees' 1970s quiet man, didn't just win a game — it ended 12 years without a pennant. As the 1976 season approached, the Yankees were enduring their longest span without a pennant since the Highlanders-turned-Yankees went 18 years before finishing first for the first time in 1921.

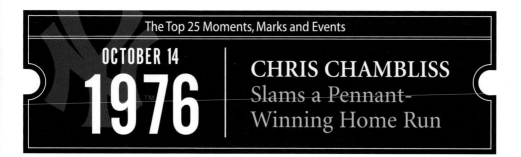

The Top 25 Moments, Marks and Events

**OCTOBER 14**

**1976**

**CHRIS CHAMBLISS**
Slams a Pennant-Winning Home Run

Over the next 44 years they won 29 pennants and 20 World Series. If you rooted for the Yankees from 1921 through 1964, your team had a two-in-three chance of winning a pennant and a 45 percent chance of winning the World Series.

Then came the collapse. Sixth place in 1965, then 10th (the Yankees' first last-place finish since 1912), then ninth. The team's slump, captured by frames of tens of thousands of empty seats in their three-tiered stadium, mirrored Mickey Mantle's decline. The collapse lasted long past his retirement in 1969. By 1976 the team inhabited a refurbished Yankee Stadium, spiritually if not physically removed from the intimidating ghosts of the Ruth-Gehrig-Huggins monuments and cavernous, unforgiving expanses in center field and left-center.

The new park promised a new start. Only Roy White and Thurman Munson remained from 1970. General manager Gabe Paul had retooled the line-up, acquiring players from the Cleveland Indians (Chambliss, Graig Nettles, Oscar Gamble), California Angels (Mickey Rivers, Ed Figueroa, Rudy May) and Pittsburgh Pirates (Willie Randolph, Dock Ellis). Catfish Hunter had signed a

landmark free agent contract in 1974. The new cast won 97 games and the American League East division in 1976.

Next up was a five-game series with the AL West champion Kansas City Royals for the pennant. The Yankees appeared to have control of the fifth game, but George Brett struck a three-run home run in the eighth inning and tied the score, 6-6. The suspense mounted as the Yankees came to bat in the bottom of the ninth, and the noisy crowd was pleading for a hero. Chambliss dug in, connected on the first pitch from Mark Littell and lifted a tantalizing fly to right field. Al Cowens sped to the fence, leaped, and stabbed for the ball with his glove. The ball eluded him by several feet, dropping beyond the 385-foot marker in right-center field.

Fans swarmed the field, intercepting Chambliss as he circled the bases. He touched second with his hand, just before a fan took the base. Third base was gone, too. Engulfed in a sea of humanity, Chambliss lowered his shoulders and broke for safety. Two hours later, under police escort, he touched the spot where home plate had been. A long, lonely period in Yankees history had come to an end.

When you think of the greatness of a group without recalling a single individual, that is the essence of team play. The 1998 Yankees won 114 games, an American League record, breaking the previous mark of 111 set by Cleveland in 1954 (in 154 games). The Yankees competed less against 29 other teams and more against a lofty standard of their own making. People who have watched baseball for decades could not recall a team that played 162 games like it expected to win them all, at least not until they saw the 1998 Yankees.

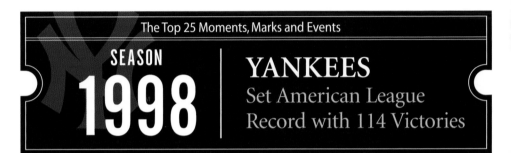

The Top 25 Moments, Marks and Events

**SEASON**

# 1998

## YANKEES
### Set American League Record with 114 Victories

No one hit 30 home runs. Only one pitcher won 20 games. No one on the roster finished in the top five in doubles, triples, homers, RBI, walks or slugging percentage. In a season of team excellence, the only league leader was Bernie Williams, who won the batting title. This wasn't the 1927 Yankees, 1961 Yankees or 1975 Reds pounding teams into submission with 38-ounce Louisville Sluggers. The 1998 Yankees played offense patiently, waiting for a favorable count to hit, waiting for walks, waiting for a mistake, waiting to make comebacks.

The strategy worked: They scored two runs more a game than they allowed. They were 20 games ahead in the standings by mid-August and won their 100th game on September 4, quicker than any other team in history.

Now immortalized, the club was constructed in a mixed way. David Wells, David Cone, Scott Brosius, Chuck Knoblauch, Tino Martinez, Jeff Nelson, Paul O'Neill, Tim Raines, Chad Curtis, Hideki Irabu and Luis Sojo arrived in trades. Mike Stanton and Chili Davis were signed as free agents. Williams, Ramiro Mendoza, Mariano Rivera, Derek Jeter, Shane Spencer, Jorge Posada and Andy Pettitte were products of the Yankees player-development system. Orlando "El Duque" Hernandez arrived from Cuba on a rickety 19-foot boat.

Twice the Yankees were tested. After they started with a 1-4 record, nervousness seeped into the clubhouse. Who might be traded or lose his job if this Rolls Royce continued to sputter? The question had hardly been uttered when they won eight in a row, then six consecutive, then eight again. By the All-Star break, the Yankees were 61-20.

The next test came in the Championship Series. Down two games to one against the Cleveland Indians, they faced the sobering thought that 114 victories might lead to nothing. Hernandez took the ball at Jacobs Field and overwhelmed the Indians. The Yankees never lost again, finishing off Cleveland and sweeping the San Diego Padres in the World Series. "We weren't Ruth, Gehrig and DiMaggio — but this is the ultimate team," Cone said.

"That kid hits them pretty far. The stratmosphere around here helps . . .

# BUT YOU STILL GOTTA BE PRETTY GOOD TO HIT THEM THAT WAY."

— CASEY STENGEL

| PLAYER | YEAR | AVG. | HR | RBI |
|--------|------|------|-----|-----|
| **Mickey Mantle** <br> New York Yankees | 1956 | .353 | 52 | 130 |
| **Ted Williams** <br> Boston Red Sox | 1942 | .356 | 36 | 137 |
| **Lou Gehrig** <br> New York Yankees | 1934 | .363 | 49 | 165 |
| **Rogers Hornsby** <br> St. Louis Cardinals | 1925 | .403 | 39 | 143 |
| **Ty Cobb** <br> Detroit Tigers | 1909 | .377 | 9 | 107 |

Major League Triple Crown Winners

Mickey Mantle's baseball career reached full bloom in 1956. He was just 24, a boy growing into a man. He ran for short bursts like an Olympic sprinter, and he had the strength of Hercules, driving baseballs to distances that amazed both his peers and his fans.

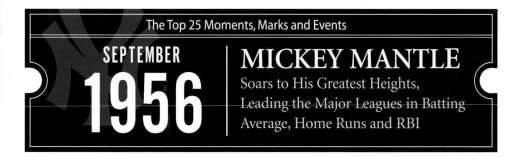

The Top 25 Moments, Marks and Events

## SEPTEMBER
# 1956

# MICKEY MANTLE
Soars to His Greatest Heights, Leading the Major Leagues in Batting Average, Home Runs and RBI

As the 1956 season coursed onward, it became apparent that the star center fielder of the New York Yankees was playing at a level above the crowd. When it was over, Mantle not only led the American League in batting average, home runs, and RBI, but he surpassed everyone in the National League as well. Mantle batted .353 with 52 home runs and 130 RBI. The only other players who have led the major leagues in all three categories are Ty Cobb in 1909, Rogers Hornsby in 1925, Lou Gehrig in 1934 and Ted Williams in 1942.

Williams challenged Mantle in the batting race, but was undone by Yankees pitchers, who limited him to 11 hits in 56 at-bats. Al Kaline fell two short of Mantle in the RBI race. Duke Snider, the closest challenger in home runs, was nine behind Mantle, who became just the seventh player in history to reach the 50-homer level.

Mantle's legend took on greater proportions on a regular basis in 1956. His greatest day of the season — perhaps the greatest day of his career — came in a May doubleheader against the Washington Senators. In the first game, he drove a ball to right field that crashed off the façade atop the third deck, failing by less than three feet to become the only ball ever hit fair out of Yankee Stadium — "The best ball I ever hit left-handed," a self-satisfied Mantle said later. Engineers estimated the ball would have traveled 550 to 600 feet had its flight not been interrupted. In the second game, he sent a drive to the base of the scoreboard in the right-center field bleachers, about 465 feet from home plate. In addition to the majestic blasts, the fleet and nimble Mantle dropped down a drag bunt that day and easily was safe at first — one of 12 drag bunts he executed that season.

His signature season continued into October. In Game 5 of the World Series, Mantle hit a home run and also got on his horse and pulled down a long drive by Gil Hodges in left-center field. All in a day's work for Mantle, but his labor on that day helped Yankees pitcher Don Larsen achieve the only perfect game in World Series history. Mantle hit three home runs in the Series, which the Yankees won in seven games against the Brooklyn Dodgers.

A crowd of more than 74,217 — another 15,000 were turned away by the fire department — began flowing into Yankee Stadium on April 18, 1923, three hours before the 3:30 start. It was the largest gathering ever to watch a major league game. Some arrived by car; most spent a nickel for subway fare.

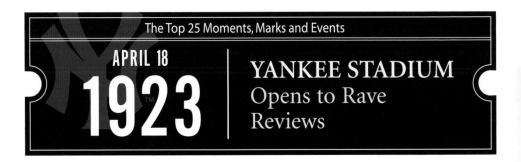

The Top 25 Moments, Marks and Events

APRIL 18

# 1923

## YANKEE STADIUM
## Opens to Rave
## Reviews

They braved a raw, breezy day to behold the grand new home of New York's American League baseball team, a triple-tiered arena shaped like a horseshoe. The upper deck was trimmed with a 16-foot copper frieze, a distinctive look that would become the Stadium's signature.

There was no venue in the world to compare to the brand new Yankee Stadium. The image of such a grand edifice, towering just off the Harlem River and visible for miles, signaled that baseball was in the chips and the Yankees were at the forefront. Babe Ruth surveyed his new digs that day and remarked, "Some ballyard, huh?"

Ruth's three-run home run christened the park, propelled the Yankees to a 4-1 victory and launched the team's golden age. The Yankees won half of the next 40 World Series, maintaining excellence over three distinct eras.

Yankee Stadium was built on 11 acres of farmland purchased for $600,000 by Colonel Jacob Ruppert, an owner of the team. The Yankees needed a place of their own because they no longer were welcome tenants at the Polo Grounds, home of the National League's New York Giants. Since the arrival of Ruth in 1920, the Yankees had steadily become the more popular team and drew bigger crowds than the Giants in the Giants' own park. Caving to the demands of his manager, John McGraw, Giants owner Charles Stoneham evicted the Yankees. "The Yankees will have to build a park in Queens or some other out-of-the-way place," McGraw said. "Let them go away and wither on the vine."

They didn't go far. Yankee Stadium was built in the Bronx, just across the Harlem River from the Polo Grounds in northern Manhattan. *The New York Times* described the new stadium as "a skyscraper among ballparks." Fred Lieb, a sportswriter of the day, was the first to call the place, "The House That Ruth Built."

As Ruth changed the look of the game by hitting the ball higher and farther than anyone else, the turnstiles spun faster at Yankee Stadium than at any other ballpark. The Yankees soon were attracting a million paying customers annually. Most teams didn't draw half that many.

Colonel Ruppert threw a party at the downtown Hotel Commodore to celebrate the opening of Yankee Stadium and crowed, "This is a wonderful occasion. I now have baseball's greatest park, baseball's greatest players and baseball's greatest team." He was right on all counts.

The most impressive thing about Babe Ruth's called shot in the 1932 World Series was that he was on the downslope of his career when he pulled it off. The Wrigley Field atmosphere that day was charged with hostility. Moments before Ruth connected, a storm of vitriol flowed from both dugouts. The torrent of emotion that fueled both the Chicago Cubs and the Yankees was about to boil over.

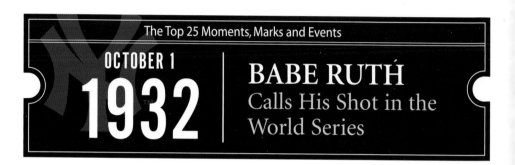

The Top 25 Moments, Marks and Events

**OCTOBER 1**
**1932**

**BABE RUTH**
Calls His Shot in the World Series

The pot started simmering during the first two games of the Series in New York. The Cubs had acquired shortstop Mark Koenig, formerly a Yankee, from the Pacific Coast League in August. Koenig played brilliantly down the stretch, yet the Cubs players voted to award him only a half-share of their World Series loot. The Yankees were livid. As the Cubs filed through the Yankees dugout to their side prior to the first game, Ruth lit into them. "Hey, you lousy bunch of cheapskates," Babe boomed. "Why do you associate with a bunch of bums like that, Mark?" After Ruth knocked nine balls into the Wrigley bleachers prior to Game 3, he sneered, "I'd play for half my salary if I could hit in this dump all my life."

The Cubs, in turn, harassed Ruth mercilessly, calling the 37-year-old "Grandpops" and making jokes about his ballooning girth. Ruth always had let the ribbing of opponents slide off his back. Even remarks from players like Ty Cobb didn't get to him. He laughed at everyone, but mostly at himself.

But this was different. This was not the Ruth of five years previous who after launching his 60th home run crowed, "Let's see some sonofabitch match that." By anyone else's standards, Ruth was still a force. But a leg injury and appendicitis had laid him up for 21 games during the season, and for the first time in seven seasons he was not the American League home run king, his 41 far behind leader Jimmie Foxx's 58. The Chicago newspapers hit below the belt, one carrying this commentary on the Cubs' opponent in the Series: "One of their outfielders is a fat, elderly party who must wear corsets to avoid immodest jiggling, and cannot waddle for fly balls, nor stoop for grounders."

The taunts continued. "By the middle of the third game, it had got just plain brutal," said Yankees third baseman, Joe Sewell. "I'd never known there were so many cuss words or so many ways of stringing them together." Standing at home plate and in the eye of the storm, Ruth audaciously held up two fingers to indicate the number of strikes, knowing that pitcher Charlie Root would have to be man enough to throw near the plate to get a third one. "I'm going to hit the next pitch down your goddamned throat," Ruth roared.

Root accepted the challenge, and Ruth drove a bent offering into the center field bleachers, the ball traveling 436 feet before landing. The game's most outsized player and beloved personality, the mythmaker without peer, had outdone his own standards for drama.

After Ruth knocked nine balls into the Wrigley Field
bleachers prior to Game 3, he sneered,

# "I'D PLAY FOR HALF MY SALARY IF I COULD HIT IN THIS DUMP ALL MY LIFE."

## Most Victories in a
## Season, 20th Century

| PLAYER, TEAM | YEAR | RECORD | PLAYER, TEAM | YEAR | RECORD |
|---|---|---|---|---|---|
| Jack Chesbro, New York Highlanders | 1904 | 41-12 | Smoky Joe Wood, Boston Red Sox | 1912 | 34-5 |
| Ed Walsh, Chicago White Sox | 1908 | 40-15 | Cy Young, Boston Red Sox | 1901 | 33-10 |
| Christy Mathewson, New York Giants | 1908 | 37-11 | Christy Mathewson, New York Giants | 1904 | 33-12 |
| Walter Johnson, Washington Senators | 1913 | 36-7 | Walter Johnson, Washington Senators | 1912 | 33-12 |
| Joe McGinnity, New York Giants | 1904 | 35-8 | Pete Alexander, Philadelphia Phillies | 1916 | 33-12 |

Jack Chesbro, whose fame followed the unpredictable path of his spitball, won 41 games in 1904 for the New York Highlanders, who would come to be known as the Yankees. No one had a clue that the 30-year-old right-hander had set a record that would hold up for the rest of the 20th Century and beyond.

The Top 25 Moments, Marks and Events

## SEPTEMBER
# 1904

## JACK CHESBRO
### Wins 41 Games —
### Most in the 20th Century

Chesbro completed 48 of his 51 starts in 1904, both records that still stand. He struck out 239, a franchise record until Ron Guidry broke it in 1978.

Chesbro was known as "Happy Jack," a nickname he picked up in his 20s while working as an attendant at a Middletown, N.Y., mental hospital and pitching for the hospital baseball team. The 5-foot-9-inch, 165-pound pitcher with an omnipresent smile arrived in New York in 1903, at the same time as the Highlanders, who had moved from Baltimore. Chesbro had gone 28-6 for the Pittsburgh Pirates in 1902 and was lured by the promise of more pay to jump to the fledgling American League.

He also was among the hardest workers in an era when pitchers routinely worked upward of 300 innings a season. He reached that level four times, peaking at an astronomical 454 in 1904.

Wee Willie Keeler's hitting and Chesbro's pitching in 1904 thrust the Highlanders into the franchise's first pennant race. Until Chesbro was knocked out of a game in August, he had pitched 30 consecutive complete games. On the final day of the season, the Highlanders trailed the Boston Pilgrims by 1½ games, and, as fate would have it, the teams were playing a doubleheader at Hilltop Park, the New York team's first home.

The score was tied 2-2 in the first game and Boston had a runner at third base with two outs in the ninth inning. Chesbro got two strikes on the batter, then unleashed a spitball that sailed over the catcher's head. The man on third raced home with the winning run, and Boston had the pennant. The Highlanders would not be a serious pennant contender again until acquiring Babe Ruth from that same Boston team in 1920.

Chesbro had several good years for the Highlanders after 1904, but they paled in comparison to his 41-12 season. He pitched until 1909 and was constantly reminded of the wild pitch he threw that eliminated the Highlanders from their first pennant race.

Chesbro died in 1931 at age 57. His widow lobbied for years to have the wild pitch officially changed to a passed ball, but her efforts were unsuccessful.

The weather was cool and misty. Babe Ruth, dressed in his old Yankees uniform with the familiar No. 3 on the back, sat in a chair in the tunnel behind the visitors' dugout at Yankee Stadium, a camelhair overcoat draped on his shoulders. When the rain subsided, he rose wearily and began his final walk onto the famous field.

The Top 25 Moments, Marks and Events

## JULY 13
# 1948

# BABE RUTH
## Makes His Final Yankee Stadium Appearance

The Yankees had marked Sunday, June 13, 1948, to celebrate the 25th year of Yankee Stadium. The crowning moment of the festivities would be the announcement that Ruth's uniform number was to be retired, never again to be worn by a player in Yankees pinstripes. Great Yankees past and present were there, and the grand ballpark had almost 50,000 seats filled. The mood, however, was somber, for everyone knew that the Babe was seriously ill. Ruth's once broad shoulders were sloped and narrow, and his cheeks that had once swelled to the size of a pumpkin with a boyish grin were now gaunt.

As the P.A. announcer introduced Ruth to a growing ovation, Bob Feller pushed a bat into Ruth's hands as the Babe struggled up the dugout steps. Feller, who was pitching for the Cleveland Indians that day against the Yankees, thought Ruth might use the bat for support. Ruth doffed his cap as he took the field. "He walked out into that cauldron of sound he must have known better than any other man," said sportswriter W. C. Heinz.

Ruth stopped along the third base line. Photographer Nat Fein of the *New York Herald Tribune*, unable to get in front of Ruth, instead snapped a photo from behind at an angle that caught the Babe in a dignified pose below the majestic sweep of the distinctive Stadium façade. It remains one of the most famous pictures in sports history.

The large crowd roared its gratitude, over and over. Will Harridge, president of the American League, conducted the No. 3 retirement ceremony. A Hall of Fame representative accepted treasure from Ruth's bounty: a uniform, glove, spikes and the bat the Babe used when he hit his 60th home run in 1927.

Finally, the Babe took the microphone. In a voice hoarse from the ravages of throat cancer, he thanked everyone for the memories and mentioned his pride in being the first to have hit a home run in the Stadium 25 years earlier. He then began a long, labored walk off the field in what to this day is known as "The House That Ruth Built," never to return. One month later, the Babe was dead.

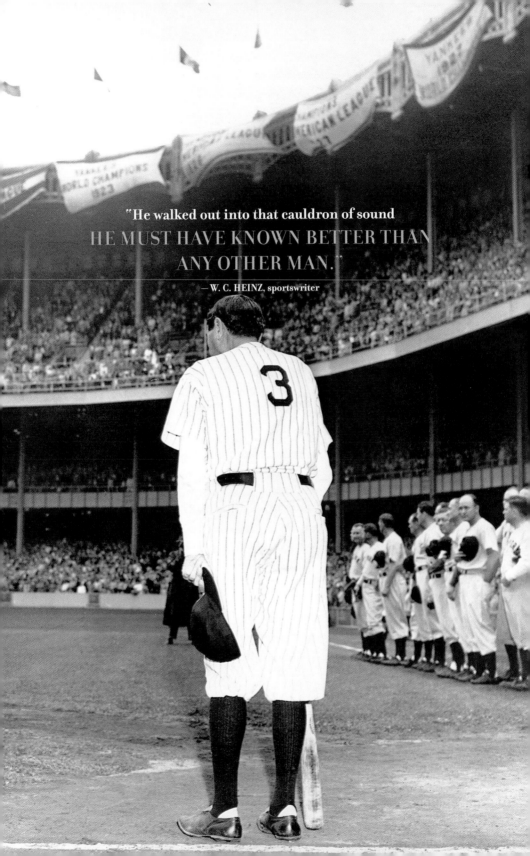

"He walked out into that cauldron of sound
HE MUST HAVE KNOWN BETTER THAN
ANY OTHER MAN."

— W. C. HEINZ, sportswriter

The Yankees of the late 1970s were consummate professionals. They routinely overcame distractions and won significant games. From 1976 to 1978 they won the American League pennant every season and twice prevailed in the World Series. Those teams had a core of talented and experienced players who truly understood how to put differences aside and play as one when they were between the white lines.

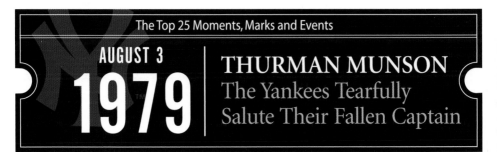

The Top 25 Moments, Marks and Events

## AUGUST 3 1979 | THURMAN MUNSON
### The Yankees Tearfully Salute Their Fallen Captain

Craig Nettles, Ron Guidry, Willie Randolph, Reggie Jackson, Chris Chambliss, Bucky Dent, Brian Doyle, Jim Beattie — superstars and obscure players alike, all had something to contribute.

The toughest of them all was Thurman Munson, the man behind the plate who ran the show. He was a block of intensity and resolve, constantly prodding for excellence. "He told me where I should play this hitter, told the center fielder where he should play, and communicated with the pitcher besides," Chambliss said. "A lot of guys looked up to Thurman's hard-nosed kind of play. With him, you just thought you were going to win."

Munson's standing among those who wore the world's most famous pinstripes became evident in 1976; the walrus-mustachioed catcher was appointed captain of the Yankees, the first to hold that position since Lou Gehrig. Munson was the American League MVP that year, as the Yankees won their first pennant in 12 years, and he hit .529 in the World Series.

A year later, Munson batted .308 and drove in 100 runs — the first AL player to achieve .300 and 100 RBI for three consecutive seasons since Ted Williams in the late 1940s. Munson was behind the plate when the Yankees won the World Series in 1977 and 1978. For his career, he batted .357 in 30

postseason games. He won three Gold Gloves for his generalship behind the plate.

Then one summer day in 1979, the Yankees captain was gone forever, dead at age 32, his major league career frozen in its 11th season. Munson was killed in Canton, Ohio, on August 2, 1979, when he crashed his private aircraft while practicing takeoffs and landings. He had purchased the plane for the convenience of commuting from New York to Canton to be with his wife and three children on days when the Yankees didn't play.

The following evening more than 51,000 turned out at Yankee Stadium and saluted the fallen captain with an eight-minute ovation. The Yankees stood on the field, heads bowed and caps in their hands. Jackson, who had his differences with Munson but greatly admired the catcher's mettle, wept openly. The Yankees announced that Munson's uniform No. 15 and his clubhouse locker would never again be used by the team.

The Yankees finished fourth in the AL East in 1979, lost to Kansas City in the 1980 AL Championship Series, and lost to the Dodgers in the 1981 World Series. What if Munson had been in the lineup for those seasons? "Had he lived," Jackson said, "I believe we would have won two more World Series, both in 1980 and 1981. Very few people have been the leader he was."

## YANKEES CAPTAINS

Hal Chase
★ 1912 ★

Roger Peckinpaugh
★ 1914 to 1921 ★

Babe Ruth
★ May 20, 1922 to May 25, 1922 ★

Everett Scott
★ 1922 to 1925 ★

†Lou Gehrig
★ April 21, 1935 to June 2, 1941 ★

Thurman Munson
★ April 1, 1976 to August 2, 1979 ★

Graig Nettles
★ January 29, 1982 to March 30, 1984 ★

††Willie Randolph
★ March 4, 1986 to October 2, 1989 ★

††Ron Guidry
★ March 4, 1986 to July 12, 1989 ★

Don Mattingly
★ February 28, 1991 to 1995 ★

Derek Jeter
★ June 3, 2003 — present ★

† Lou Gehrig died on June 2,1941
†† Named co-captains on same day

The 2001 World Series offered something new for the Yankees, difficult as that was to imagine, considering that they were playing on baseball's biggest stage for the 38th time, more than any other two teams combined. Down two games to one to the Arizona Diamondbacks, the Yankees tied Game 4 with a home run in the bottom of the ninth inning and won with a home run in the 10th.

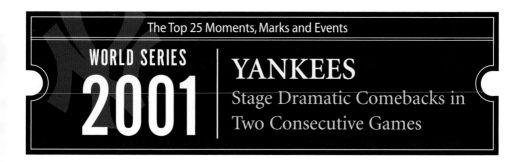

The Top 25 Moments, Marks and Events

**WORLD SERIES 2001** | **YANKEES**
Stage Dramatic Comebacks in
Two Consecutive Games

It was the first time in 97 World Series that such a that scenario had played out. A day later, the Yankees continued their unbelievable performance. Again they tied the score with a home run with two outs in the bottom of the ninth then won in extra innings.

From the time President Bush threw out the ceremonial first pitch for Game 3 at Yankee Stadium until Chuck Knoblauch scored the decisive run on Alfonso Soriano's hit in the 12th inning of Game 5, baseball offered grief-stricken New Yorkers a chance to celebrate the city's undaunted spirit and valor. In the seven weeks since the attack on the World Trade Center, the Yankees and the Mets had provided welcome relief for New Yorkers in need of a diversion from real-world issues.

The upstart Diamondbacks had a 3-1 lead with two outs in the bottom of the ninth inning of Game 4. It had been a miserable Series for Yankees hitters, who had managed but a .143 average against Arizona pitchers. The Yankees had a runner on base, and Tino Martinez was the batter. Byung-Hyun Kim, a 22-year-old sidewinder from

Korea, tried to sneak a belt-high fastball past Martinez, but Martinez sent the ball into the night and over the center field fence, tying the score. Fifteen minutes later, Kim failed again, delivering a 10th-inning gopher ball to Derek Jeter that left the Yankees improbable 4-3 winners.

As if they were Broadway thespians, the Yankees staged a repeat performance less than 24 hours later. Kim again was on the hook for the Diamondbacks with two outs in the ninth inning, charged with holding a 2-0 lead. Again he caved, his offering dropped over the left field fence by Scott Brosius. An hour later, Soriano drove home the decisive run with a single. On consecutive nights, the Yankees had overcome two-run deficits in the ninth inning and won — an achievement equaled only four previous times in the World Series.

The Series ran its course in the Arizona desert, and the Yankees had no magic remaining for the final two games. The Diamondbacks won the war — but the two battles won by the Yankees in stunning fashion were symbolic of a great city that refused to be conquered.

The 1953 World Series was a chance for the Yankees to scale still another level of greatness. They had been the dominant team in majors since the 1920s. From 1936 through 1939 they won every World Series; no other team had ever won more than two straight.

*Hank Bauer, Yogi Berra, Billy Martin and Joe Collins (left to right) celebrate after the Yankees win the first game of the 1953 Series.*

# WORLD SERIES
# 1953

## BILLY MARTIN
### Leads the Yankees to an Unprecedented Fifth Consecutive World Championship

From Ruth to Gehrig to DiMaggio, the Yankees wove a tapestry of excellence. DiMaggio retired after the 1951 season; after the team won the World Series for the third consecutive year. There would be no break in the chain. Mickey Mantle stepped in as the next larger-than-life presence on America's greatest team. The Yankees beat the Brooklyn Dodgers in the 1952 Series, and the same teams were the last ones standing again in 1953. Someone calculated the odds of one team winning every World Series from 1949 to 1953 — an unprecedented five straight — at 1,048,576 to 1.

Long odds never applied to the Yankees, though the same can't be said for the hero of the 1953 Series. Mantle, Yogi Berra and Phil Rizzuto were bound for the Hall of Fame, yet none ever had a Series to match Billy Martin's performance in 1953. Martin was a career .257 hitter who drifted through seven teams in his 11 years in the major leagues.

He was best known for his combative and cantankerous personality, and for his escapades with best-friend Mantle. Martin rose far above his journeyman station in the 1953 Series, batting .500 and delivering 12 hits, a record for a six-game Series. His final blow was a single up the middle of the diamond in the bottom of the ninth inning of the sixth game. It brought home the decisive run, ended the Series, and gave Martin 23 total bases for the Series. "When I crossed first base and realized that we had won it, a thousand sensations seemed to pass through my body all at once," Martin said. "You

did it kid! — that's what I kept telling myself over and over again. But I just couldn't believe it."

Twelve players shared in the five consecutive World Championships: Berra, Rizzuto, Hank Bauer, Jerry Coleman, Joe Collins, Ralph Houk, Eddie Lopat, Johnny Mize, Vic Raschi, Allie Reynolds, Charlie Silvera and Gene Woodling. Players come and players go, and in the Yankees' case, those coming always were equal to those they were replacing. DiMaggio, Tommy Henrich and Joe Page departed; Mantle, Gil McDougald and Whitey Ford arrived.

The Yankees had grown so mighty that it had become fashionable to root against them. Emanuel Celler, a U.S. congressman from Brooklyn, claimed the Yankees were a monopoly and protested in a verse published in *The New York Times*, a day after the 1953 Series ended. The musical *Damn Yankees* hit Broadway in May 1955 and ran for 1,019 performances — on stage, at least, the Yankees could be beaten.

Few doubted the Yankees could win again in 1954. "The Yankees, as they are now constituted, have a good chance to win the pennant in 1954 — unless the other clubs get stronger," said Casey Stengel, their astute manager.

Indeed, the Yankees won big in 1954, claiming 103 victories, their best total since 1942. But it was good for only second place; Cleveland won 111, the American League record at the time. A year later, the baseball world was back to normal: The Yankees won the pennant, the first of four in a row.

It was Yogi Berra Day at Yankee Stadium. The pregame ceremonies honoring the greatest catcher in Yankees history ended with Berra behind the plate, receiving the ceremonial first pitch from Don Larsen, a reprise of sorts of that October 1956 afternoon when Larsen pitched the only perfect game in World Series history.

The Top 25 Moments, Marks and Events

## JULY 18
# 1999

# DAVID CONE
## Pitches the 14th Perfect Game of the 20th Century

hen the old teammates and almost 42,000 fans settled in for a ballgame between the Yankees and the Montreal Expos. As the innings passed by on Sunday afternoon, July 18, 1999, Berra and Larsen must have glanced at each other on occasion in wide-eyed amazement. For out on the mound, David Cone was retiring the Expos 1-2-3, without incident, inning by inning.

It was Cone's 14th season, and he had not won a game in nearly three weeks. Cone had ridden great talent to great heights. He had won 177 games, struck out 19 in a game, nearly pitched a no-hitter in his first start after recovering from surgery to repair an aneurysm in his right arm. He had pitched in four World Series, won eight postseason games. Now Cone was 36, and his fastball had lost its hop. He had to rely more on guile and gumption, and a variety of pitches thrown at varying speeds and from different arm angles. Once asked about his chances of making the Hall of Fame without having 200 wins, Cone, who would finish his career with a 193-123 record, replied confidently, "It's the quality of the stats, not the quantity, that counts."

On this Sunday afternoon, Cone was crafting a performance of quality that would have been rare for a pitcher in his prime, much less a 36-year-old of faded glory. Though Montreal held an unimpressive place in the standings, the result might have been the same had Cone been facing the best team of Berra's era. Cone kept the Expos' hitters on the defensive, getting ahead in the count with breaking pitches that bent impossibly and following with fastballs that painted the corners. This approach was so effective that by the sixth inning Orlando Cabrera, the ninth batter in the Expos' order, had reached a dreaded conclusion. "I'm going to be the last out," Cabrera told a teammate.

Cone had his closest call in the eighth inning. Jose Vidro lashed a grounder that appeared headed for center field, but second baseman Chuck Knoblauch fielded the ball on his backhand and made the throw to first base in time. Finally it was Cabrera's turn in the ninth. The 27th batter lifted a popup that nestled into the glove of third baseman Scott Brosius for the 27th out.

David Cone had pitched the 14th perfect game of the 20th Century. And there to witness it were the pitcher and catcher of the greatest perfect game in history. Only the Yankees could pull off such high drama.

Three days short of his 35th birthday, in "The House That Ruth Built,"
Wells had accomplished a feat that had eluded all but 12 others,
INCLUDING HIS IDOL.

David Wells once said he could never pitch a no-hitter because he threw the ball over the plate too frequently. Wells was wrong. On the afternoon of May 17, 1998, he not only pitched a no-hitter, but the 13th perfect game of the 20th Century. Wells befuddled the Minnesota Twins with fastballs and sharp-breaking curves thrown with precise control. His idol would have been proud of him.

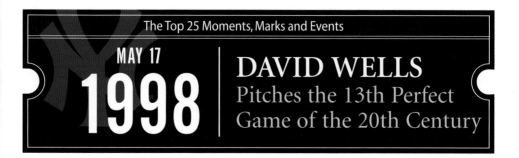

The Top 25 Moments, Marks and Events

**MAY 17**

# 1998

## DAVID WELLS
### Pitches the 13th Perfect Game of the 20th Century

Wells was a great admirer of Babe Ruth. Though separated in age by more than 60 years, the two had much in common. Both were accomplished left-handed pitchers, had round faces, portly physiques, mischievous grins, and were noted free spirits. Wells once took the mound for the Yankees wearing a flat cap that Ruth had worn in the 1920s, and he asked if he could wear uniform No. 3 in honor of the Babe. The request was denied, so Wells settled for No. 33.

When he took the mound against the Twins that May day, Wells was a pitcher merely trying to find his way. His work had been inconsistent. Two starts previous, he had surrendered most of a 9-0 lead and didn't finish the game. The Yankees manager, the ever-optimistic Joe Torre, tried to buoy Wells' confidence and spirit, mentioning that the lefty had ability enough to pitch a no-hitter.

Sure enough, Wells found his pitching rhythm against the Twins and began a high-level game of pitch-and-catch with Jorge Posada. Wells went to a three-ball count with only four batters. He struck out 11, and his fielders made no exceptionally tough plays.

As is the custom when a pitcher has gone deep into a game without giving up a hit, the Yankees did not mess with Wells in the dugout. Nobody wanted to jinx him — ridiculous, maybe, but a time-honored tradition. Torre did joke to pitching coach Mel Stottlemyre after the seventh inning that Stottlemyre ought to inform Wells he was through for the day and the bullpen would finish up. The always chatty David Cone was the only player who spoke to Wells, suggesting, with as straight a face as he could muster, that Wells try out the knuckleball he had been working on.

Wells spent the bottom of the eighth inning sitting alone in the dugout, stretching his neck and arms. The Yankee Stadium crowd of 49,820 afforded him a standing ovation as he left the dugout to pitch the ninth inning.

Wells got two outs in routine fashion. The last batter was Pat Meares, who swung late and hit a lazy fly to Paul O'Neill in right field. The crowd grew quiet for a moment and then roared as O'Neill made the catch. Wells pumped his arm madly as the Yankees swarmed him in celebration near the pitcher's mound. Three days short of his 35th birthday, in "The House That Ruth Built," Wells had accomplished a feat that had eluded all but 12 others, including his idol.

Two strikes on Bobby Grich. Ron Guidry backed off the pitcher's mound at Yankee Stadium and onto the grass, making him look 5-feet-8-inches tall instead of the official 5-feet-11-inches. At either height, he was a reed with pipe-cleaner legs. He stretched his arms mightily and swung them in a starfish motion.

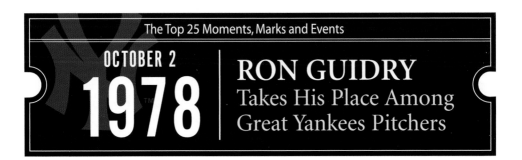

The Top 25 Moments, Marks and Events

**OCTOBER 2**

# 1978

# RON GUIDRY
## Takes His Place Among Great Yankees Pitchers

Ready to pitch again, Guidry climbed back atop the mound to growing, rhythmic clapping from fans anticipating what was about to happen. Guidry rocked into his motion and let go a slider that approached home plate at belt-level, then dove suddenly. Too late for Grich to react; his swing was a foot above the ball. It was June 17, 1978, and Guidry was crafting one of the finest pitching performances in Yankees history. He set a club record that night by striking out 18 batters.

Every aspect of pitching came easily for Guidry in 1978. He had nine shutouts, a Yankees record and the most in the major leagues by a left-hander since Babe Ruth pitched nine in 1916. Guidry won his first 13 decisions, and by the time the season had run its course he had a 25-3 record, a winning percentage of .893, the best of all time among 20-game winners.

Guidry edged aside several Yankees greats in 1978. His 248 strikeouts was a team record, breaking the 74-year-old mark of Jack Chesbro, who had 239 strikeouts and a 1.82 ERA in 1904. The previous best winning percentage for a Yankees 20-game winner was held by Whitey Ford, who went 25-4 (.862) in 1961.

Guidry's 1.74 ERA was the lowest for a major league left-hander since Sandy Koufax's 1.74 in 1964 and 1.73 in 1966. Unlike Guidry, Hubbell didn't face a lineup that included a designated hitter. The DH has increased American League run production by about half a run a game. Adjusting ERAs accordingly, no one since Bob Gibson in 1968, who had a 1.12 ERA, has been as stingy as Guidry.

Guidry's victories in 1978 had pennant-race implications, too. The Yankees once trailed the Boston Red Sox by 14 games but made up the gap, and the teams met in the famous playoff game decided by Bucky Dent's home run.

Guidry pitched three shutouts in September, two against the Red Sox in a week. He kept the Yankees alive with a 3-1 win over the Toronto Blue Jays on September 28, and after three days' rest he was on the mound in Fenway Park for the game to decide an American League East champion. With a little help from Dent, he won his 25th game that afternoon.

# BEST WINNING PERCENTAGE FOR 20-WIN SEASONS

| PLAYER, TEAM | YEAR | W-L | PCT. |
|---|---|---|---|
| Ron Guidry, New York Yankees | 1978 | 25-3 | .893 |
| Lefty Grove, Philadelphia Athletics | 1931 | 31-4 | .886 |
| Preacher Roe, Brooklyn Dodgers | 1951 | 22-3 | .880 |
| Fred Goldsmith, Chicago Cubs | 1880 | 21-3 | .875 |
| Smoky Joe Wood, Boston Red Sox | 1912 | 34-5 | .872 |

1.74 GUIDRY'S ERA IN 1978

248 GUIDRY'S STRIKEOUTS IN 1978

Under Steinbrenner's rule,
THE FAMED PINSTRIPED UNIFORM AGAIN WOULD COME TO
REPRESENT SUSTAINED EXCELLENCE.

On January 3, 1973, a limited partnership headed by George M. Steinbrenner III as the managing general partner purchased the Yankees from the CBS television network. The most famous team in professional sports had fallen on hard times, but the change of ownership righted the pinstriped ship.

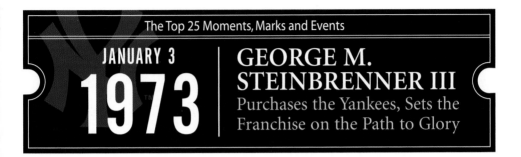

## JANUARY 3
# 1973

## GEORGE M. STEINBRENNER III
Purchases the Yankees, Sets the Franchise on the Path to Glory

Within four years, prudent trades and player acquisitions from the free-agent market had rejuvenated the team. The Yankees returned to freshly renovated Yankee Stadium in 1976, and a year later won the World Series for the first time in 15 years.

Steinbrenner's group paid $10 million for the Yankees, $3.2 million less than CBS paid for the franchise in 1964. The performance of the Yankees from 1965 through 1972 — they finished no higher than third in those years — was the chief reason for the reduced price. "I think CBS suffered some small embarrassment in buying a club at its peak and then having it fall from first place in the league, to sixth place (1965), and then to 10th (1966). The bottom fell out," said Michael Burke, Yankees president from 1966 to 1973.

The 1972 Yankees had made a spirited run, only to falter and finish fourth in the American League East. Their low place in the standings was not the only troubling reality. Yankees attendance in 1972 fell to 966,000, the first time since 1945 that the team had fewer than one million spectators. Steinbrenner, though, hardly was deterred. Rather, he saw buying into a franchise that had won 29 pennants and 20 World Series in the 45 years from 1920 to 1964 as an opportunity of gigantic proportions. "It's the best buy in sports today. I think it's a bargain," he said at the time.

Steinbrenner grew up in Cleveland, an Indians fan, but he appreciated the buzz that accompanied the Yankees wherever they went. "When the Yankees came to town, it was like Barnum and Bailey coming to town," he said. "It was the excitement. Being in Cleveland, you couldn't root for them, but you would boo them in awe."

The Steinbrenner era began with finishes of fourth, second and third in the standings. Then came a pennant in 1976, achieved in dramatic fashion when Chris Chambliss cracked a home run in the bottom of the ninth inning of the final game of the Championship Series.

Under Steinbrenner's rule, the famed pinstriped uniform again would come to represent sustained excellence. Dynasties in Major League Baseball were expected to go the way of the dinosaur when the rule that enabled teams to control player movement was struck down in court. Yet through 2003, 31 years under Steinbrenner's stewardship, the Yankees had won 10 pennants and six World Series. The next most successful Series teams during that span were Oakland and Cincinnati, each with three World Championships.

The ball shot off Mickey Mantle's bat on a screaming line. It soared beyond the left-center field fence at Griffith Stadium in Washington, D.C., high above the 391-foot marker. The ball ticked a football scoreboard mounted atop a 50-foot-high wall that stood 69 feet behind the outfield fence and soared onward.

The Top 25 Moments, Marks and Events

## APRIL 17 1953 | MICKEY MANTLE'S 565-Foot Home Run

When the ball struck pavement, it bounced over a two-story building and finally came to rest behind a house at 434 Oakdale Street, a block from the stadium. Donald Dunaway, a 10-year-old boy who had seen the ball clear the stadium, ran to pick it up.

Yankees public relations director Red Patterson left the stadium to find where the ball landed. As the story goes, he then calculated the distance as best he could, by taking into account the acknowledged measurements inside the stadium and pacing off the rest of the distance. His estimate was 565 feet, though no one knows for sure where fact left off and fiction took over.

A man with a name eminently suited for comic-book fame, Mickey Mantle was 21 when he crunched that ball beyond the sight lines of everyone inside Griffith Stadium on April 17, 1953. Over the next 15 years, from both sides of the plate, he would strike blows just as famous and perhaps just as far. But this one helped launch the Mantle legend.

Mantle was bigger than that game, and he would transcend games to come. The towering blast in the nation's capital afforded baseball fans a glimpse of what this muscular kid from Oklahoma could do. Of all Mantle's talents that contribute to his mythic stature as an American hero, none was greater than his awe-inspiring ability to make a ball disappear into the far reaches of the sky.

A report in *The New York Times* the following day said Mantle's home run was the longest in major league history, except for one hit by Babe Ruth in Detroit's Navin Field, in 1926, that traveled 600 feet. The distance of Ruth's clout was not measured, though several witnesses swore to it in an affidavit. The newspaper also mentioned a 587-foot shot by Ruth during a 1919 exhibition game in Tampa.

The boy who found Mantle's 565-foot home run ball gave it to Patterson in return for money, and Patterson gave it to Mantle. The curator of the Hall of Fame asked Mantle for the ball to display it in Cooperstown, and Mantle agreed. Mantle hit his most famous homer with a bat borrowed from teammate Loren Babe, and that, too, was sent to the Hall of Fame.

565
FEET
GRIFFITH STADIUM BLAST

*(left to right) Mickey Mantle, Bobby Richardson, and Whitey Ford*

126

The Yankees had won 19 World Championships and were on the verge of another. All they had to do was protect a one-run lead in the bottom of the ninth inning in the seventh game of the 1962 World Series at San Francisco's Candlestick Park.

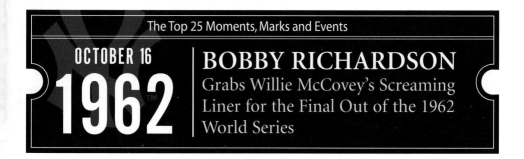

The Top 25 Moments, Marks and Events

**OCTOBER 16**
# 1962

## BOBBY RICHARDSON
Grabs Willie McCovey's Screaming Liner for the Final Out of the 1962 World Series

The Giants had challenged the Yankees relentlessly throughout the Series, and well they should have. Willie Mays was in his prime, and he'd been joined in the San Francisco lineup by young sluggers Orlando Cepeda and Willie McCovey. All three ended up in the Hall of Fame.

The Series lasted 13 days, which included a four-day rain delay between games five and six. Four games were played in Candlestick Park, a wind tunnel that whipped fly balls into spinning dervishes chased with great uncertainty by harried outfielders. Pitcher Stu Miller once was blown off the Candlestick mound by a sudden gust in the dead of summer.

Candlestick's unpredictability and Ralph Terry on the mound were the cause of great uneasiness for Yankees fans as the Giants came to bat in the ninth inning, trailing 1-0. Terry was a 23-game winner that season, yet just two Octobers previous he had yielded Bill Mazeroski's seventh-game, ninth-inning homer in Pittsburgh that had won the Series for the Pirates.

Matty Alou led off with a bunt single. Terry got two outs, then Willie Mays sent a line drive toward the right field corner. Roger Maris cut off the ball before it reached the fence and threw a quick relay to Bobby Richardson. Alou made third, but he certainly would have scored if not for Maris' nifty work in right field. Mays was at second.

Next up was the menacing McCovey, a powerful left-handed hitter who would clout 521 home runs in his career. First base was open, but in a lively conversation on the mound, Terry convinced Yankees manager Ralph Houk that he could retire McCovey with "good stuff just outside the strike zone." Richardson, the second baseman, moved a yard toward first base from where he normally played and ignored Houk's gesture to assume his usual position. McCovey's bat met Terry's third pitch flush, as a gun discharging a bullet. The ball shot on a screaming line toward right field, only to slam into Richardson's glove at chest level. "A yard to one side or the other and I wouldn't have had a chance at that ball," Richardson said.

Candlestick fell silent, except for the celebratory exchanges among the Yankees on hostile ground. Terry tossed his glove and cap into the air, and his teammates lifted him atop their shoulders and carried him off the field. The Yankees had repelled another challenge to their supremacy and gained a hard-earned World Championship—the 20th for the storied franchise.

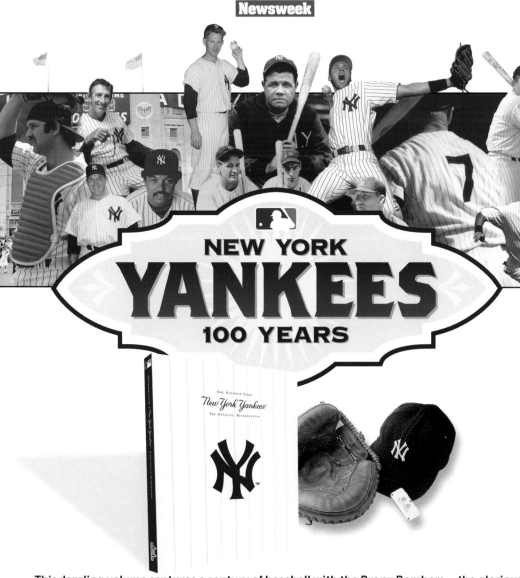